Books by Nigel Rees

In hardback

"Quote...Unquote"
The "Quote...Unquote" Book of Love,
Death and the Universe
'Quote...Unquote 3'
Graffiti File
Slogans

In paperback

Babes and Sucklings
Eavesdroppings
Foot in Mouth
Graffiti Lives, OK
Graffiti 2
Graffiti 3
Graffiti 4
"Quote...Unquote"
"Quote...Unquote 2"
Very Interesting ... but Stupid!

NIGEL REES

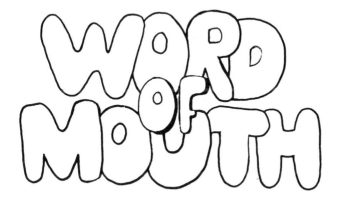

WORD OF MOUTH

BOOK CLUB ASSOCIATES
LONDON

Eavesdroppings first published in Great Britain
by Unwin Paperbacks 1981

Foot in Mouth first published in Great Britain
by Unwin Paperbacks 1982

Babes and Sucklings first published in Great Britain
by Unwin Paperbacks 1983

This edition published 1983 by Book Club Associates
By arrangement with George Allen & Unwin Ltd

Eavesdroppings © Nigel Rees Productions Ltd 1981
Foot in Mouth © Nigel Rees Productions Ltd 1982
Babes and Sucklings © Nigel Rees Productions Ltd 1983
Word of Mouth © Nigel Rees Productions Ltd 1983

Word of Mouth is based on the three paperbacks *Eavesdroppings*,
Foot in Mouth and *Babes and Sucklings*. *Foot in Mouth* was
designed by *The Small Back Room*.
The three illustrations reproduced on the jacket are taken from
the three paperback books and are by Korky Paul.

British Library Cataloguing in Publication Data

Rees, Nigel
    Word of mouth.
    1. English wit and humour   2. Bulls, Colloquial
    I. Title
    828'.91407'08   PN6231.B8
    ISBN 0-04-827092-X

Printed in Great Britain by
Butler and Tanner Ltd, Frome and London

Illustrated by
Chris Winn

Whenever two people are gathered together and a third is hovering a yard or so away – there you have the makings of an 'eavesdropping'. This book is a compilation of the more peculiar of the species.

It has been made possible through the wildly enthusiastic response from listeners to my BBC Radio programme *Quote . . . Unquote.* The present collection of a few hundred of their overhearings is the mere winnowing of several thousands we have received. It seems that almost everybody has at least one such remark that he or she treasures.

Now, although I use the word 'eavesdroppings' to describe these fag-ends of conversation, I do not wish to imply that they were gathered illicitly. True, the dictionary defines 'eavesdrop' as the water that falls from the eaves of a house and 'eavesdropper' as someone who stands close to a house – 'within eavesdrop' – to hear what people are saying. But the fact is that eavesdropping in public is something that it is virtually impossible to avoid without turning down your deaf-aid. There is a certain type of person – American tourists traditionally top the list, closely followed by those 'two old ladies on a bus' – who is so unselfconscious that bizarre outpourings rain upon the innocent bystander.

7

There are certain locations, too, which make escape from overhearing more or less impossible – even if you wanted this to be so: tops of buses (the most likely place), park benches, cinemas, theatres, restaurants, hospitals and pubs, crossed telephone lines. Stand still for a minute or two in Stratford-upon-Avon (or any other major tourist centre) and you are bound to hear a few. Every ten years, the performances of the Oberammergau passion play produce a good crop. The blackout during World War II concentrated people's hearing wonderfully.

If I was to define the best type of eavesdropping it would be one whose context was impossible to fathom and one where the identity of the speaker was not known. This would, unfortunately, rule out an example of the genre told to me by Iwan Williams (who was one of the first to suggest that *Quote . . . Unquote* might concern itself with what he called 'aural graffiti'). 'When you and I were both at Oxford,' he says, 'I passed through the Kemp café one day bearing coffee and perceived someone we both know staring deeply into the eyes of a young lady and saying, "You know, the first girl who ever seduced me wore contact lenses, too".'

One or two manufactured jokes have also, I am sure, crept into this book. On the other hand, I do not think that there are a lot of deliberate inventions. There are so many bizarre things to be overheard in real life as to make this unnecessary. There is a tendency for people to claim that they personally have scraped up an eavesdropping when really they are quoting somebody else's. So where an attribution is made it may mean no more than that this was the person who sent in the remark.

8

I have tended to exclude overheard remarks from children and I could have included many more straightforward double entendres ('Yes, she actually did it on the stairs, you know'; 'Henry, put your thing in your other hand', etc.). The same applies to malapropisms, though one of these – 'I know I'm right because I got it by word of earmouth' – is so inspired I have used it as a chapter heading.

The subject-matter of these eavesdroppings covers the whole range of human experience with special emphasis, it sometimes seems, on physical infirmity and cremations. The most amusing tend to arise when people are so busy wrestling with their thoughts that they fall over the language. The results range from the touching to the ridiculous, from the curious to the downright ignorant. Occasionally there is a nice piece of folksy perception among these 'whirls of pisdom' (as they were once described to me) and I personally find something warmly pleasurable in contemplating these brief flashes of existence preserved in aspic.

Some of the eavesdroppings have been savoured by their hearers for many years. One of the oldest and best known is about the sudden quiet passage in a piece of music which enabled a whole concert audience/church congregation/group of nuns to overhear one of its members say to another, 'Well, we always fry ours in lard.' That has been around since the last century, though people quote it as if it was said yesterday. I suppose it *was* actually said once?

Another such came to me from Paul Fincham, of Suffolk, who heard it from Paul Jennings who had it from Alfred Deller, the late counter-tenor. Mr Deller, it appears, was walking behind two ladies when he heard one say to the other, 'Ow's Flo? Ow's 'er feet?' The second lady replied, 'Well, of course, they're not much use to 'er now. Not as *feet*, that is.'

On the other hand, perhaps Alfred Deller was not the first to hear this remark. Some of these 'eavesdroppings' must have been broadcast over loudspeakers at mass rallies, so many people claim to have overheard them personally. These are the ones I style *'Traditional'*.

One reason for this phenomenon is that the passing on of overheard remarks is a venerable activity. The old *Westminster Gazette* used to publish them under the name of 'conversation lollies', I'm told. Newspaper exposure has made them part of popular folklore. However, the vast majority included in this volume are original and I think this is the first collection of its size there has ever been.

10

My thanks are due to all the people who have contributed to these pages and who have given permission for me to reproduce their eavesdroppings. I hope those we have been unable to trace will nevertheless enjoy seeing their little gems in print. I am also indebted to David Higham Associates for permission to quote from *Ruling Passions* by Tom Driberg (Cape, 1977) and to Hughes Massie for permission to quote from Agatha Christie's *Autobiography* (Collins, 1977).

So, long live some of the best comedians we have – other people. May they never discover how funny they are!

WORD OF MOUTH

'There is nothing like eavesdropping to show that the world outside your head is different from the world inside your head.'

Thornton Wilder,
The Matchmaker

If you have ears, prepare to shed them now

I was walking by the Serpentine in Hyde Park with two office colleagues one lunch-hour and we overheard a very puzzling remark. Two young men passed us, deep in conversation, and one of them was making the intriguing observation:

'What he didn't know was – her mother had a bike.'

Alec Mowbray, Bognor Regis

13

Two ladies passed me outside a shop. One said to the other:

'When I do it, I tend to catch my fingers on the floorboards.'

Sarah Lewis, York

I have cherished this since my earliest days at Cambridge:

A: **'He's a strange man . . . very strange . . . '**
B: **'What do you mean, strange?'**
A: **'Well, he's not** *like* **any other Tibetan lama I've ever known.'**

Dr Valerie J. Males, London N16

While in the National Gallery viewing the voluptuous picture *The Rape of the Sabine Women* by Rubens, a little old lady nearby turned to her friend and said:

'I suppose it's their jewels they're after.'

Mildred Barratt, Reigate

My mother once overheard one of two women passing her say:

' "Well," I says to him, I says to him, I says, says I, "Well, I says," I says.'

Capt J. M. A. Wilson RN, Chichester

Winn.

'What he didn't know was —
her mother had a bike.'

Overheard on the train:

> *First commuter:* **'I suppose you've heard that Joan and John have separated.'** *Second commuter:* **'You know, I did wonder when I saw John going down the road without his wig on.'**

Mrs M. C. Pierce, Offham

Christopher Matthew, the novelist and journalist, reports a conversation overheard in a restaurant. An elderly man who had sat with a slightly younger woman in total silence for almost the entire meal suddenly declared, 'Do you know that the corridors of the Hermitage in Leningrad when added together come to twenty-seven miles?' The woman said:

'Shut up and get on with your fish.'

In the days of silent films I was once in an Edinburgh picture-house watching a thriller. Behind me were two elderly ladies, one of whom was reading aloud the subtitles to her companion. As the situation reached its climax, in the silent suspense, came the subtitle, and then the voice:

'The thick plottens.'

Mrs Dora Thomas, Edinburgh

Overheard in a hospital examination cubicle:

Doctor: '**Now, Mrs Jones, bend the knee please.**'
Mrs Jones: '**Which way, doctor?**'

J. M. McKenzie, Peterborough

Overheard beside a swimming pool in Singapore:

'**You made that dress yourself. Goodness, how clever!** *(Slight pause)* **Why didn't you use a pattern?**'

Mrs Bridget Kelly, Old Beaconsfield

I didn't know whether to laugh or cry when I overheard the following between two old dears on a Reading bus:

A: '**Hullo, dear, haven't seen you about for a long time.**'
B: '**No, I've been in hospital for six weeks – rushed there with me heart.**'
A: '**Oh, that was bad. How did Fred take that then?**'
B: '**Oh, he's been ever so good. He really has. He made me a lovely little shed right outside the back door so I don't have to carry the coals all the way from up the garden.**'

Mrs D. E. Kleboe, Othery

17

My mother always maintained that she really did hear an irate woman on Southsea beach saying to her small son:

'Alfie, come here you naughty boy. Will you have smack bottom now or the other thing when you get home?'

Revd Canon John Hayter, Lymington

I overheard this in a cafe. Two ladies were sitting quietly, then one said:

'It's a funny thing about that man . . . he's been married three times and all his wives were called Ethel.'

Mrs M. Duff, Ilkley

A classic eavesdropping was collected by Gilbert Harding when, having arrived at a restaurant well after last orders had been taken, he persuaded the staff to find him something to eat. Just as he was digesting the morsel he overheard one waiter saying to another, incredulously:

'He's eaten it!'

Two old ladies stood shivering in the bus queue.

First lady: **'Isn't the weather dreadful?'**
Second lady: **'Yes, but it's better than nothing.'**

Mrs P. M. Packham, Hornsey, London N8

'... to carry the coals all the way from up the garden.'

This is a comment my wife and I heard from a motorist who was consoling a friend whose tyre was somewhat deflated. We heard him say:

'It's only the bottom, the top's all right.'

Mr and Mrs A. R. G. Dutton, Staines

My local theatre put on a production of *Macbeth*. At one performance the auditorium was full with a party of OAPs. When she heard the line, 'Tomorrow and tomorrow and tomorrow,' one old darling turned to her friend and said:

'That makes Thursday.'

Jonathan Wallace, Rochester

While I was a Housemaster at Eton, my wife and I were walking round Agar's Plough on 4 June, when we heard a lady in front saying:

' . . . and as he'd had a long run down, he asked for the bathroom. When he was shown into it, he suddenly looked and there was his hostess in the bath. He couldn't think what was the correct thing to say, so he said, "You *are* looking well".'

C. D'O. Gowan, Ulverston*

---

* Douglas Sutherland, author of the *English Gentleman* books, advises that the correct thing to say was: 'I beg your pardon, sir!'

In a hotel restaurant in rural Gloucestershire in 1971, two elegantly dressed elderly ladies at the next table were discussing an acquaintance. One said:

'I'm not exactly sure what he does, my dear, but it's something to do with cows.'

Philip A. J. Culver, Tewkesbury

'There are only two in the whole of Guildford and one is covered in ants.'

Traditional

21

This is part of a conversation between two lady cleaners at the London theatre where I used to work:

> *A:* '**I see that woman died then.**'
> *B:* '**What woman?**'
> *A:* '**The one that went out with the fellow that had the boat.**'
> *B:* '**Boat? What boat?**'
> *A:* '**You know the one. Then he married the other woman who shot the President.**'
> *B:* '**Oh, she's dead is she?**'
> *A:* '**No! The other one. Oh, what's her name ... um ... Mary, um ... Mary Callas! That's her.**'
> *B:* '**No. Don't know the woman.**'
> *A:* '**Yes, you do. She used to sing** *rather loud.*'

Ronald Price, London W4

I overheard two ladies discussing an old man who had had both legs amputated. Between the 'Ohs' and 'Ahs' one lady said:

'Yes, same two as Bader.'

Phyl Longstaff, Cambridge

I was shopping in Woolworth's when two young assistants passed me on their way upstairs for their tea break. One said to the other:

'Well, why don't you like blokes wiv airy ear'oles then?'

Mrs Laura Leggatti, Twickenham

22

'There are only two in the whole of Guildford and one is covered in ants.'

As you can tell from his brilliant vocal feats, Kenneth Williams has given close study to the way people talk and what they have to say. On a bus he heard one woman say to another:

'We don't have any more trouble now because I get the cut loaf and he puts the marge on himself.'

On another occasion, Kenneth heard two men outside a London club:

'I've just been to Evita,' *said one. To which the other replied:* **'You don't look very brown.'**

I overheard two lavender-scented old ladies on Fellows' Day at the Chelsea Flower Show. One said to the other:

'Now my head gardener is dead, I'll be able to let you have some treasures from the greenhouse.'

Mrs W. P. Howard, Buxton

My bus picked up two old ladies at the hospital gates:

A: **'Well, luv, there y'are.'**
B: **'Ay, yer see, it would've been all right if it'd been** *round.* **It were the fact that it were** *oblong* **that did it.'**

Mrs Jessie Parry, Doncaster

24

Heard on the top of a double-decker bus several years ago when I was sitting behind two girls in their late twenties:

> **'It's all very well for people to tell us young girls that some day your prince will come, but when he's been and gone you've had it.'**

Betty Pilditch, Dibden Purlieu

Two elderly ladies were overheard as they sat talking on a park bench. One said:

> **'When one of us passes on, I shall move south to live with my daughter.'**

Traditional

I overheard this remark on a West Midlands bus: One lady to her friend:

> **'I had my husband cremated – but it was a mistake.'**

Mrs Josephine Hayes, Cheylesmore

I went to a Writing for Pleasure class and we were told to eavesdrop on conversations and save them for future use. On the way home on the bus, two elderly ladies were discussing one of their daughters, aged thirty-five, and unmarried. Her mother was justifying:

> **'Why bother to marry? She has her Dad and me and her tropical fish.'**

Mrs Barbara Kimber, Bristol

'Why bother to marry? She has
her Dad and me and her
tropical fish.'

Overheard outside the Gents' lavatory on the Foreshore at Scarborough:

Small boy: **'Daddy, why are we going here?'**
Father: **'To get away from your mother.'**

David Sillito, Scarborough

My wife and I were sitting in the cinema when a trailer was being shown for the Bob Hope – Bing Crosby film *The Road to Utopia:*

Young lady behind us: **'Mary, where is Utopia?'**
Mary: **'I'm not sure, but I think it's in the Mediterranean.'**

Alfred Brooks, Reading

I overheard this in a shopping precinct said by one of two women standing in a shop entrance:

'Yes, I saw her yesterday. She was panic-buying pot plants.'

Julia Lang, Southsea

Here is an eavesdropping collected at a Sheepdog trial in the Peak District:

A: **'Oh, hello Ann. How lovely to see you again. And how's John now?'**
B: **'Well, he still has to stand sideways.'**

R. Mahony, Potters Bar

WORD OF MOUTH

This was overheard by my stepfather,
Mr W. S. Knight, in the public library at Bury St
Edmunds. One old lady sat reading a
newspaper and was approached by another
old lady who asked, 'Excuse me, but is it
Wednesday or Saturday today?' To which the
first replied:

**'I couldn't tell you dear, I'm a stranger
here myself.'**

P. C. Edwards, Peterborough

A friend of mine was walking in Bury St
Edmunds behind two girls. A lady on the other
side of the road waved to the girls but
apparently they did not know her because my
friend heard one girl say (in broad Suffolk):

**'Why do her wave to we? Us don't know
she.'**

Miss N. Green, Sudbury

From *The Journal of a Disappointed Man* by
'W. N. P. Barbellion', first published in 1919 –
what may be the original of a much-overheard
remark:

7 August 1915: **'On the bus the other day
a woman with a baby sat opposite, the
baby bawled, and the woman at once
began to unlace herself, exposing a
large, red udder, which she swung into
the baby's face. The infant, however,
continued to cry and the woman said,
"Come on, there's a good boy – if you
don't I shall give it to the gentleman
opposite".'**

'He still has to stand sideways.'

The lady in front of me in the queue at a small corner store asked the girl at the check-out (in a marble-mouthed voice): 'How much are your toilet rolls, dear?' When told, she replied:

'Oh, that's too much for what I want them for.'

Brian Thompson, Newcastle-upon-Tyne

I heard the following from a woman at the adjoining table in a department store's restaurant in Ealing:

'It's a year this week since my poor husband died. Oh, I do miss the car.'

F. P. Brown, Salisbury

I passed two young women wheeling a pram up the High Street. One remarked to the other:

'... and as the frog died when she had her pregnancy test, she's going to call it Froggy ...'

Vicki L. Bergen, Bromley

Overheard coming out of the upper window of a cottage on a bright summer morning in a small Oxfordshire village:

'Will, do ee want the use of my body afore I put on my corsets?'

Marie H. Standish, London NW3

Overheard in a crowded Edinburgh bus –
gaudily overdressed woman at the back shouts
to man in the front:

> **'What time is it, Jeremy, by your** *gold*
> *watch?'*

Ivor Malcolm, Oban

Overheard on a Bournemouth bus:

> *First girl:* **'They have so many dogs! All**
> **over the house . . .**
> *Second girl:* **'Oh, I don't like dogs in the**
> **house. But horses, now, that's quite**
> **different.'**

F. Wilson, Plymouth

Some years ago entering Stonehenge, I
overheard a harassed mother say to her small
daughter:

> **'Now, Doreen, just you be careful and**
> **don't knock anything over.'**

L. Markes, Brockenhurst

Lady to two friends, overheard in a café in
Cardiff:

> **'And when I got home, Action Man had**
> **moved all the rhubarb.'**

Brenda Ray, Mickleover

'Action Man had moved all the rhubarb

Eavesdroppers hear no good of themselves

Mollie Parkin, the novelist, was about to appear on a Welsh TV programme when she overheard two female members of the audience discussing the panellists. About herself she heard:

'She writes very rude books and is always overdressed.'

A young artist saw an eminent critic and a noble lord standing in front of one of his paintings, so he crept nearer to hear what they were saying about it. The noble lord said to the critic:

'Of the two, I prefer washing up.'

Traditional

The scene – the members' enclosure at Henley Regatta. This was spoken by an excited young lady, dressed to kill, on catching sight of what lay on the far side of the crowd. In an excruciating upper-class accent, she said:

'Oohhh! I didn't know Henleh was on the rivah!'

Outside the Whittington Hospital in London, two departing middle-aged female visitors were talking. One said to the other:

'Yes, dear. She was the only one in the family to 'av 'em. One on top and one underneath.'

A. V. Sabourin, Ashford

Overheard at the Oberammergau passion play in 1934 (when I was 14). It lasts from 8 a.m. to 6 p.m. with a two-hour break for lunch. About 4.30 p.m. an American in front of us said, 'Let's go, I've had enough!' The reply:

'I'd like to stay and see how it finishes.'

Peggy Gardner, Swansea

34

Overheard in a pub near Catterick:

'And I hope she doesn't start blowing her bubbles until I've finished my act.'

Miriam Stanton, Newby

I overheard a rather exotic old lady in a shop saying to another:

'Well, my favourite saint is the one who looked after all the birds and the animals. What was his name – Francis of Onassis?'

David Bennett, Hitchin

Overheard in Leeds, delivered in a rich Yorkshire accent by a man who looked as if he might be a foreman in one of the local works:

'I can't tell my blokes what to do any more – I 'ave to *motivate* them.'

Cyril Wilson, Harrogate

I have a friend who lived above a marriage bureau which was run by a large, formidable county type of lady. One day he heard her booming voice saying to some poor persistent wife-searcher:

'I am afraid there is not much demand for small Maltese gentlemen.'

J. Lamps, London SW1

35

' I'm afraid there is not much demand
for small Maltese gentlemen. '

Coming out of a revival of *My Fair Lady:*

'And yet I find it very hard to understand why it is they can't find an actor to play Professor Higgins who can *sing.'*

K. H., Ruislip

John Mortimer, the playwright and QC, was in the crush bar at the Royal Opera House, Covent Garden, just before a production of *Don Carlos*, conducted by Giulini, directed by Visconti, and starring Placido Domingo. In came a 'Hunting Henry' character who asked loudly of his companion:

'What are they givin' us tonight, darlin'? Singin' or dancin'?'

Overheard by a friend – circumstances beyond recall.

Woman: **'It was so quiet, you could have heard a mouse drop.'**

David Lennox, Penistone

Travelling by train to the West Country, the lady and gentleman sitting opposite me had obviously been to the Chelsea Flower Show. Eventually they began to discuss their own gardens:

Gentleman: **'Have you any ducks on your lake?'**
Lady: **'Only on the small one.'**

Miss Helen Pates, Waltham Cross

Overheard in a small general shop:

> *Gentleman customer:* **'Do you sell Valentine cards?'**
> *Lady shopkeeper:* **'Yes. Is it for a man or a woman?'**

Miss R. M. Kaye, Bishop's Stortford

Two old ladies in the local market place. One said:

> **'Well, I've told her before about using my toothbrush, and now see what's happened.'**

Judy Beckett, Coventry

Overheard in Bedford town centre:

> **'They can't be living in sin – she wears a frilly apron.'**

B. A. Witton, Bedford

Like most authors, P. D. James, the crime fiction writer, keeps her ears open for useful snatches of dialogue. Whether she will ever be able to use this one is open to question. In the village store of a village in Dorset, she heard one local woman say to another:

> **'Her be that old, all the fluff do be coming out of her woollies.'**

'... only on the small one!'

'Her be that old, all the fluff do
be coming out of her woollies.'

There is a Chelsea pub which has a large vine
growing in the courtyard. One summer the
vine produced a good harvest of grapes, which
the landlord made into wine. A particularly 'far
back' Sloane Ranger was given some to taste
and, being unable to spit, swallowed.
Stonefaced, she asked the landlord, '*Where*
did you say this came from?' 'Out there,' he
replied, pointing to the courtyard. Said she:

'Hum, doesn't travel well, does it?'

Fiona and Alan Francois, London N1

On top of a London bus, girl enthusing to
friend about recent honeymoon:

**'It was a lovely place and they were ever
so nice people. They said we could use
their bathroom, but as we were only
there for five days we didn't like to
bother them.'**

John Doxat, London W8

Overheard on a Sheffield bus outside the
Royal Infirmary:

**'Yes, I've been visiting George and it's
like a miracle. The doctor says they've
pumped all the blood out of his body,
boiled it up, and pumped it back in again
– and he's coming home on Wednesday.'**

Miss M. R. Schofield, Monkton Heathfield

WORD OF MOUTH

I had a day in Herm recently and while I was sitting by the path, a family came along with a little boy of five or six hanging back a little. Suddenly Dad turns to him and says:

'If you don't stop whining, Margaret Thatcher will come and get you.'

Mrs Winifred Lusty, Guernsey

I overheard the following conversation on the District Line. Two elderly cockney ladies were discussing the ailments of various members of their families:

First lady: **'And what about Arthur?'**
Second lady: **'He's better now but he had the most horrible injuries, you know.'**
First: **'So I heard, but how exactly did he get them?'**
Second: **'It was when he was in the RAF. He fell over a WAAF in the dark.'**

Mrs M. F. Lloyd Davies, Saffron Walden

In a long and successful career as a theatre director, Peter Dews has had ample opportunity to collect overheard reactions to his own productions. After *Vivat! Vivat Regina!*, which he directed at Chichester and which ends with the execution of Mary Queen of Scots, he overheard a female member of the audience say:

'Do you know, it's extraordinary – exactly the same thing happened to Monica.'

At that moment the train arrived, so I'll never know...

Sheila Burnford once wrote a short story which appeared in the May 1959 issue of *Blackwood's Magazine* and told of a woman travelling by train who overhears an isolated remark and then becomes obsessed with trying to discover its meaning. Eventually her husband starts worrying over it too. The phrase in question is:

'Poor Albert floated when he died . . .'

Mrs Burnford comments: 'The story originated out of a game that a friend, Jill, and I used to play when we were young and travelling in trains. The game was to maintain a conversation not too suspiciously outrageous (yet sufficiently earnest and straightfaced) for the benefit and reaction of our fellow travellers in the compartment. For example, I might say something like: "I always wondered why Anthony *insisted* on cleaning his with that appalling stuff he brewed up on the Aga." To which Jill might answer: "Well, Belinda once said that was why Nell cleared off – she couldn't stand one more bucket of newts dripping all over the larder." And off we would go from there. We developed a fine sense of audience reaction – the book or newspaper pages that hid the face but remained unturned, the pseudo-sleeper, and once, just once, an elderly man who must have played the game himself. As he left the carriage, he turned and said something like "What an enjoyable journey", then, devastatingly, "My brother-in-law thinks that he lost all his shallots to a neighbour's baboon this year." He left us, for once, speechless.

I cannot remember now how we worked up to it but it was definitely Jill's voice that came out with the poignant remark that "Poor Albert floated when he died". The story of Albert was the first I ever wrote, nearly twenty years later. He certainly altered my life and gave me a career, for then I wrote *The Incredible Journey,* which became a best-seller. Throughout the years he has been strangely with me, for I keep running into people even now who have read about him, and are still wondering themselves what befell him.'

44

I am not at all sure as to how the avoidance of ending a sentence with a preposition is regarded today, but I was once sitting on the top deck of a No. 27 bus at Highgate, listening to two ladies arguing in the front seat about a book which apparently one had lent to the other. One of them became very cross and said:

'Then why did you give it to me to read out of from for?'

H. G. Knights, Ipswich

The following overheard remark struck me as so bizarre that I feel the need to specify exact time and place as an earnest of its verity – Place: Market Square, Cambridge. Date: 28 August 1979. One American to another:

'It was when he took his glass eye out that I saw the resemblance to mother.'

Simon Sedgwick-Jell, Cambridge

45

'It was when he took his glass eye out that I saw the resemblance to mother.'

I heard a gardener talking to a friend about another gardener with whom he had once worked:

> '**He** *was* **a greedy man, the greediest man I ever saw. One day at teatime, he ate half a cucumber, and I ate the other half.**'

C. E. Lailey, Bexhill-on-Sea

Overheard at the opera – a performance of Mozart's *Don Giovanni*. Two women meet in the foyer:

> *First woman:* '**Hello, fancy seeing you here!**'
> *Second woman:* '**Oh, I love this sort of thing. I saw the** *Sound of Music* **six times.**'

H. Powell Lloyd, Findon

I heard a woman on a bus some years ago saying to her friend:

> '**In your ear! I don't believe it.**'

David Fowler, Warwick

In the busy High Street I was hurrying to pass some women when I heard one say to the other:

> '**Yes, she had to have her leg off right down to the foot.**'

Mrs Alice Gallant, Market Harborough

WORD OF MOUTH

I heard this eavesdropping in a coffee lounge at Butlin's, Clacton:

'I don't actually believe in the Resurrection, but I do think there's something going on up there.'

Mrs Marion Rilstone, East Barnet

During a recent military exercise, I overheard the following brief given by a major to a private:

'You are to stand by the fire doors. When I ring the fire alarm, you will allow nobody to leave, explaining that it is not a fire – it is just a nuclear attack.'

A. Green, Canterbury

Overheard in Blandford Forum, Dorset – I was on the top of a stationary bus, the voices were on the pavement below:

First lady: **'Did you get caught in the rain, Doris?'**
Second lady: **'Not really – it wasn't bad enough to come in out of from.'**

J. W. Pinney, Stone

I overheard the following remark passed between two women in an Oxford store:

'You know the day I mean, dear. The one after Christmas Eve.'

Robert Main, Aylesbury

'She had to have her leg off
right down to the foot.'

WORD OF MOUTH

Two people sheltering in shop doorway:

> *She:* 'Hello. You haven't been to see me lately.'
> *He:* 'No, I've been busy, you know . . . '
> *She:* 'Well, do come again soon – I'll take my teeth out next time.'

> *Charles W. Edwards, Evesham*

In a snack bar in Florence we overheard an American boy of about ten say in wonder to his mother:

> **'Gee, Mom – they've got pizzas in Italy, too.'**

> *Gerald and Valerie Mars, London NW3*

A couple were gazing up at York Minster. The man said reverently, 'It's very old, isn't it?' She replied:

> **'Mm, yes. It's been there as long as I can remember.'**

> *Mrs Gillian Rastrick, Long Marston*

A teashop somewhere in Chelsea. During a slight lull in the gentle buzz of conversation, we were startled to hear a lady's cultured but rather strident voice saying:

> **'You can imagine how she felt when Mother's ashes fell in the canal.'**

> *G. L. Parkes, Birmingham*

Overheard in a very plush hotel dining-room where four prosperous-looking gentlemen were lunching together:

'I always hide mine in the greenhouse and my wife never finds them.'

Mrs M. E. Dash, Cranleigh

When I was at grammar school during the late 1920s we had a visit from the poet Walter de la Mare. He told us about a bit of eavesdropping he had done on a bus. One girl was saying to another (and as she was a cockney, the glottal stop operated, almost entirely cancelling the sound of the letter 'k'):

'I like 'er, but I don't like 'er like I like Lil.'

Mrs Betty Crowe, Broxbourne

On a Bristol bus:

'He's a funny little dog, you know. He likes beer but not bottled beer.'

Millicent Crowther, Darley Abbey

Overheard on a bus – a middle-aged Welshwoman, saying:

'I don't smoke, I don't drink, but I do love my jumble-sales – you've got to have something.'

Miss Jennie Wilkins, Hemel Hempstead

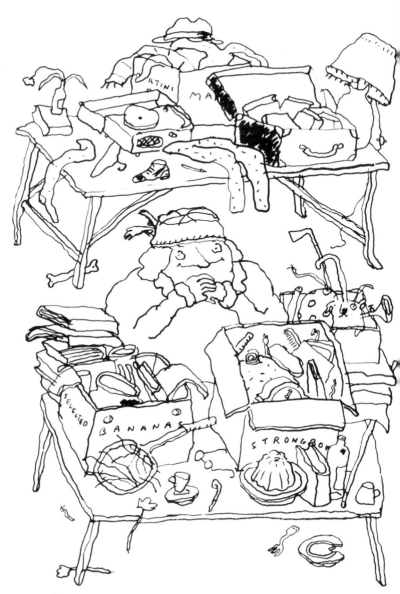

'... I do love my jumble sales —
you've got to have something.'

As I passed by a bus queue I overheard one young lady telling her friend:

'My mother lost hers at a garden fête in front of the vicar.'

Miss M. Forester, Bookham

The following exchange was heard in a country post office in North Norfolk. The postmaster said, 'Good morning, Mr Jackson, nice to see you again. How are you today?' Mr Jackson replied, 'Very well thanks. I've called to collect my pension. The postmaster:

'Yes, of course. Do you have any means of identification?'

Ron Olsen, Horning

Overheard in the local confectioner's shop:

A: **'Wasn't it terrible about that hotel disaster in Spain?'**
B: **'Oh, yes, terrible, and there's nothing worse than being killed on yer 'olidays.'**

Mrs Amy Otterwell, Oldham

Pete Atkin, the writer, collected an eavesdropping from a conversation between two elderly ladies on the bus. 'I tell no lie,' he says. 'They were discussing their families and one said, "How's your daughter?' And the other one said,

'Oh, fine. She's still writing books. Autobiographies mostly."

Overheard on a bus:

> **'I'm not sure where he is now, but it's either West Hartlepool or the Gold Coast.'**

F. D. Mason, Hexham

At a performance in English of Richard Strauss's opera *Salome* at the Leeds Grand Theatre, Salome danced, Herod asked what she demanded, Salome repeatedly asked for John the Baptist's head, and during a momentary pause in the frenzied music a lady was heard whispering to her neighbour:

> **'*What* did she say she wanted?'**

Michael Meadowcroft, Leeds

Overpaid, overfed, oversexed and overheard

I was walking past the statue of Achilles in Hyde Park – the one where he is defying the lightning – and two American ladies were admiring it. One said to the other:

'No, dear, Big Ben is a clock.'

Norman Mitchell, Weybridge

I was sharing a table with two charming old ladies. One of them said:

'I don't want to be bad friends with her. I wish you would telephone and tell her. You see, if I telephone, she won't answer.'

Mrs Evelyn Moon, St Osyth

My mother and I were visiting the very fine collection of Greek and Roman statues at Holkham Hall in Norfolk. As.we passed a totally nude statue of the god Hermes, I heard a Lancastrian lady behind me saying to her friend:

'Isn't that like the man that reads the news.'

Revd J. Butterworth, Dudley

Paris 1945. Two American GIs examining a notice saying 'Défense d'uriner':

'No, I guess it only means this particular piece of wall.'

James Atkins, London NW1

Overheard whilst looking at the Taj Mahal by moonlight, having gone at this time expressly to catch the magical moment:

'If this had been in America it would have been floodlit.'

Mrs G. Fulton, Barnston

'There was I on a Sunday morning up to my waist on the bed of the Thames and my sister not half married.'

Traditional

Once at the Edinburgh Festival I sat next to two very genteel elderly local ladies at a performance of *Pericles* which opened on a stage strewn with mirrored cushions and beaten brass tables. 'Where is it supposed to be?' whispered one. Said the other, 'Egypt – a brothel in Alexandria.' Declared the first:

'Och, it's *nothing like* a brothel in Alexandria.'

Norman Bain, London SW18

Two women were sitting behind me on a bus talking together when one of them broke off in mid-sentence and exclaimed in tones of annoyance, 'Look, I'm doing it again!' Whereupon her companion said:

'I should put a spot of oil on and put a little wire brush down.'

Mrs E. Dixey, Leicester

I gathered this eavesdropping in our local High Street.

Mother to child: **'Of course we don't need sausages, we've got Mr Robinson.'**

Mike Dennis, Clacton-on-Sea

My mother-in-law told of a phrase overheard on a bus in Huddersfield, spoken by a portly woman to her equally portly husband who in true northern fashion had got on the bus first. As they sat together, she said:

'Move over, Daddy, I've only got one cheek on.'

Mrs Enid Grattan-Guinness, Barnet

Anna Ford, the broadcaster, once heard two girls in a Glasgow store having a wonderful conversation about what had happened to them the night before. 'I only caught the tail end of it,' she says, 'and I've never worked out what it meant.' One of the girls remarked:

'So I said to him, "Get that thing out of my body!" '

Overheard in the blackout:

'But, darling, men do it so much better.'

Mrs J. A. Keyser, Coventry

As they walked through the main shopping centre in Norwich two days before Christmas, one young girl said to another:

'I give up. I'm going to give Grandma one of those dribbly things.'

Mrs Sheila Peal, Cringleford

'Of course we don't need sausages, we've got Mr. Robinson.'

Overheard on the top of a bus. One old lady to another:

> **'Of course, he took his dog collar off first . . . '**

Mrs Elizabeth Montague, Sidcup

Overheard in the bus:

> *First young teenager:* **'Jimmy walked me home from the shops last night. I don't like him much.'**
> *Second ditto:* **'Neither do I – he's only after one thing.'**
> *First ditto:* **'Yes, I know, he's always cadging your fags.'**

Mrs Peg Watson, Heddon-on-the-Wall

Overheard at the lunch table:

> **'I'd advise you to hurry up and get your vasectomy done before it goes up again.'**

Mark Bertinat, Great Sutton

Overheard by the waterlily pond in Kew Gardens:

> *First Birmingham woman:* **'The goldfish are lovely, aren't they?'**
> *Second ditto:* **'Yes, but the trouble with goldfish is when you're swimming among them, they suck yer arms.'**

Di Seymour, London NW3

'one of those dribbly things.'

'The trouble with goldfish is
when you're swimming among them
they suck yer arms.'

Overheard in a motorway service café, a young German enthusiastically telling his obviously impressed girlfriend:

'We were going so fast down the autobahn the window-cleaners fell off.'

D. E. Davies, Christchurch

I heard a lady say to her friend:

'Yes, but fancy him using a rasher of bacon for a book mark.'

Joyce Rogers, London E2

During the war I had arrived a bit early at a rendezvous at Larkhill, Salisbury Plain. It was late evening, dark and very quiet, and I was just standing waiting. Two soldiers walked past quite close and as they receded into the distance, I heard the words:

'The break-up came when she gave me bloody Bob Martin's Condition Powders.'

Col D. E. Newton, Nazeing

A man and woman were hurrying out of a big department store when the woman said severely:

'Well, you'll just have to go on drying your feet on a towel, that's all.'

Miss P. Manser, Maidstone

I was walking along the pavement in St Helier when a man behind me rushed up to a man in front and said:

'I'm sorry. I made a mistake. I buried the *live* one and not the dead.'

Frances Le Sueur, Jersey

The biographer, Robert Lacey, was in a Bristol cinema with his wife, Sandi, watching the film *Women in Love*. At the conclusion of the memorable scene in which Alan Bates and Oliver Reed wrestle with each other totally naked and then lie exhausted on the carpet, they overheard a lady behind them remark:

'Nice carpet!'

Overheard during an interval of *The Mastersingers* at the Coliseum:

First gentleman from NW4: **'Ah, Mr Greebaum, I told my wife that we shoult see you at Meistersinger.'**
Second gentleman from NW4: **'But, of course, Mr Goltstein, I alvays come to Meistersinger. I haf seen it many times in Dresden beffore the troubles, I haf seen it in Vienna and Bayreuth and at Covent Garten, but I like it best here becoss, ass they do it in English, you can onderstandt ivery vort they are singging.'**

Alan Stabell, Barnet

'Well, you'll just have to go on
drying your feet on a towel, that's all.'

Overheard some years ago in Leicester market, one woman to another:

'My second had a lovely leg.'

Kate Watts, Leicester

We took our children to the London Zoo on a very, very hot day. The smell in the hippopotamus house was almost indescribable. As we left the building, two teenage children were approaching. When the wave of nauseous odour hit them, they clapped their handkerchiefs over their noses and one exclaimed:

'Coo! Talk about my dad.'

P. Date, Sawston, Cambridge

My eavesdrop dates back to the Coronation in 1953. Two women were overheard discussing the television coverage. 'Wasn't it all beautiful?' one said. The other replied:

'Yes, what a pity the King didn't live to see it.'

E. Moore, Birmingham

A little girl in a shop in Hobart, Tasmania, one December was heard to say. 'Mummy, look at all those presents, is it someone's birthday?' Mother replied:

'No dear, it's Christmas.'

Suzanne Palmer-Holton, Princes Risborough

This was overheard by me many years ago in High Holborn and never forgotten. I walked past two men, one of whom was saying:

'. . . and instead of having it in the usual way he had it under my wife's arm.'

E. G. Aust, Newcastle-upon-Tyne

Scene: the Snowdon Mountain Railway on a beautiful summer afternoon. Two elderly ladies in print frocks, flowery hats and beach-bags full of picnic things were chatting happily and confidentially. Other sounds ceased and I clearly heard one of them say, in a gently Welsh voice:

'That's why we aren't having the funeral this afternoon.'

Sylvia Clark, Paisley

Kenneth Williams was in a bus queue near Broadcasting House when he heard this memorable – and curious – speech by one woman to another:

'I was at their housewarming. There was no room at all. We were forced to stand – literally – by the stairs . . . and it was then that I saw it, lying there. And luckily Muriel had some cotton wool and she put that round it. And I had a napkin and we covered it with that. And left it there. And for all we know, my dear, it's lying on those stairs to this day.'

WORD OF MOUTH

One handyman at a party was overheard
saying to another:

**'Have you tried doing it underwater
with a pair of scissors?'**

Michael Grendon, Stroud

A woman sitting behind me on a bus said to her
companion:

**'Of course, *we* should say that she was
peculiar, but *they* call it nerves.'**

Miss Barbara M. R. Northrop, Leeds

I dialled a telephone number and obviously got
a crossed line:

Woman: **'The doctor had a look at it,
then he had a feel of it – then he cut it
off.'**
Man: **'It's surprising how quickly it
heals.'**

Mrs Joan M. Burgess, Harwich

Remark overheard in a cloakroom and
treasured ever since. One teenage girl to
another:

**'All of a sudden he said, "I want to
marry a virgin", so I got straight up out
of that bed, got dressed and went home.'**

Mrs C. M. Brown, Cheltenham

' And for all we know, my dear,
it's lying on those stairs to this day. '

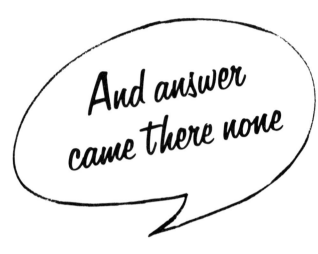

And answer came there none

A party of Americans was being shown round Jesus College, Cambridge. After some whispering among them, a spokesman diffidently addressed the guide:

'Er – excuse me – er – can we – er – see the *actual* room?'

Richard Feachem, Southampton

At a country auction, two women behind me in the crowd were talking about books. One said:

'That Lady Chatterley's Lover's not worth reading. There's nowt wot we a'nt done.'

Mrs Eric Cooper, Retford

Overheard in an Edinburgh cinema during the film *Airport 77* when a man, apparently a doctor, is tending those injured in an accident. Eventually, he confesses that he is not really a doctor, but a vet. Said a voice behind:

'He'll probably shoot the one with the broken leg.'

Mrs Margaret Harkness, Loanhead

At the most riveting moment of a film the woman behind me turned to her neighbour and said:

'I 'ad a lovely sitting of ducks come off yesterday.'
Mrs C. Baggott, Much Birch

Overheard in our Dublin local – two men talking. One said to the other:

'You could use up fourteen bags of sawdust before you could reach the crutch.'

Mrs L. Brown, Dublin

Mark Bunyan, the entertainer, says that since he heard this remark over five years ago he has been disturbed and unsettled by the picture which was conjured up! Two men were having a conversation behind him which ended:

'And you have no idea how difficult it is, actually, to get a budgerigar out of a treacle tart.'

71

'And you have no idea how difficult it is, actually, to get a budgerigar out of a treacle tart.'

Overheard in Ealing – two ladies talking. One said to the other:

'Well, I don't know what he's got to grumble about, she's been very nearly faithful to him.'

Elizabeth Veale, London W13

On the top of a bus going along Oxford Street
two cockney girls were sitting in front of me
and as we passed a cinema one turned to the
other and said:

>'I don't fancy that, d'you?'
>'Wha'sat?' replied the other.
>'Richard the 'underdf and elevenf.'

Tony Vincent Isaacs, London NW3

I overheard the following on a bus:

>*First man:* **'I'm off home to write to the
>Income Tax.'**
>*Second man:* **'Having trouble are you?'**
>*First man:* **'They want to know what
>relation my mother is to me.'**
>*Second man:* **'What are you going to tell
>them?'**
>*First man:* **'Going to tell them she's my
>Aunty Joyce.'**

Jenny Alston, Accrington

I overheard this remark in a café at St Davids,
Pembrokeshire:

>**'There were quite a lot taking
>communion and I was at the end of the
>row. I could see the chalice was getting
>empty and I was going to get the dregs
>at the bottom. So I said to myself, "Sod,
>you vicar, I will keep my lips closed,"
>and that's what I did.'**

D. Ll. Williams, Llanon

Overheard in Boots. Lady with husband in tow to shop assistant:

> **' 'E says 'e's got a buzz in 'is yer [ear], but I put my yer 'ole by 'is yer 'ole and I didn't 'ear no buzz.'**

Iris Pouteaux, Gurnsey

I overheard a woman talking to her friend at a bus-stop in Halifax:

> **'And I told 'er. I sed, you enjoyed it goin' in – you mun enjoy it comin' aht!'**

Yvonne Salcombe, Hebden Bridge

Overheard as two ladies were walking along the village street. The elder to the younger:

> **'Well, if I were you I wouldn't buy your dress yet because by the time you get married, it probably wouldn't fit you.'**

Miss H. B. Vernon, Hyde

One old lady to another:

> **'Yes, she had him cremated and his ashes made into an egg-timer.'***

Traditional

---

* Of which the equally traditional conclusion is :'Well, he never did any work while he was alive, so he might as well do some now he's dead.'

'So I said to myself, "Sod you, vicar. I will keep my lips closed," and that's what I did'

My daughter overheard two women at the bus-stop here in Barrow. One said, 'I don't like this new North Sea gas at all.' The other agreed:

'Neither do I, I can always tell when the tide is out because the flames go low, and when it's in they come up high again.'

Mrs Dorothy Armer, Barrow-in-Furness

In her posthumously published autobiography, Agatha Christie mentioned how an overheard conversation helped start one of her earlier novels:

> 'I considered writing another book. Supposing I did – what should it be about? The question was solved for me one day when I was having tea in an ABC. Two people were talking at a table nearby discussing somebody called Jane Fish. It struck me as a most entertaining name. I went away with the name in my mind. Jane Fish. That, I thought would make a good beginning to a story – a name overheard at a tea-shop – an unusual name, so that whoever heard it remembered it. A name like Jane Fish – or perhaps Jane Finn would be even better. I settled for Jane Finn – and started writing straightaway . . . it became *The Secret Adversary*.'

Overheard in Oxford:

> 'And there it was – a trail of bird seed all the way to the Psychiatry Department.'

Mrs O. Longstaff, London SE10

Outside an ecclesiastical tailors near Westminster Abbey, two ageing vicars:

> A: 'And how is your wife?'
> B: 'I never had one. But my mother is well, though getting older.'

Sarah Laughton, Plymouth

76

In New York I went to see a very prestigious production of Ibsen's *Wild Duck*. Behind us were a plump, well-heeled, middle-aged American couple. The wife asked, 'Are you enjoying this dear?' The husband said, 'Oh, sure, dear, it's fine.' The wife persisted, 'Now, dear, I don't think you really like it, do you?' The husband:

'Well, honey, to be truthful, I was going by the name and I thought it was going to be a leg show.'

Barbara Spry, East Hoathly

During the war I was having tea one afternoon in Daly's restaurant in Glasgow. Behind me two women were talking, and suddenly, in a brief moment of quietness, the words of one of them rang out clearly:

'My dear, can you believe he'd be so inconsiderate – my husband has sent me *another* salmon.'

Miss Esmé Murray Speakman, Taynuilt

I was walking up Whitehall after leaving my office in the Ministry of Defence when I espied a woman talking crossly to her dog. When I came up close I noticed the dog was wearing a particularly sullen expression. When I passed them, the woman was saying:

'Don't just stand there arguing.'

Lt-Col G. L. Shadwell, Chislehurst

77

I heard this on top of a Leeds tram in about 1949:

> **'It's all right going on your holidays, but when you get back home, your dishcloth's as stiff as buckram.'**

Mrs M. Bradshaw, Leamington Spa

The following was overheard on a bus:

> *First woman:* **'We're going to the amateur operatic tonight.'**
> *Second woman:* **'How nice. What are they doing?'**
> *First woman:* **'Well, I'm not sure, it's either** *Brigadoon* **or** *Lorna Doone.'*

Irene Miller, Bamford

Girl, aged 16, had told her parents she wanted to go on a fortnight's camping holiday with her boyfriend on his motorbike. She was asked, 'What did they say?'

> **'Mummy said it's all right as long as I take a crash helmet.'**

Mark Miller, Buckfastleigh

I heard this in the street as a couple passed my shop:

> **'It makes it so much easier to commit suicide – Mrs Jones had a big bosom like that, you see.'**

Mrs Pat Parris, Llandrindod Wells

'Don't just stand there arguing.'

Overheard on the no. 37 bus

Two old ladies overheard on a bus just after the introduction of decimalisation:

'I think they should have waited until all the old people were dead.'

F. H. Fry, Southampton

Two elderly ladies overheard on the bus.

A: **'See that church over there – that's where Bill and Lil got married.'**
B: **'Who?'**
A: **'You know, Bill and Lil. Those two who are getting divorced.'**

Miss Phyllis Allsop, Stanmore

Overheard on a bus. A woman said, 'Well, he came home so upset. He'd seen two dead ferrets in the road.' Her friend commented, 'Poor love. How upsetting for him.' So the first one said:

'Yes it was, but I told him, "You should have brought one home. I've never seen a ferret".'

Mrs D. F. Peim, Swindon

Overheard in a local shop after a minor road accident:

A: **'Who was hurt?'**
B: **'You know that chap who worked at Camell Laird's?'**
A: **'Was it him?'**
B: **'No, but his friend had a daughter and it was her husband's brother.'**

Mrs B. Elizabeth Ely, Birkenhead

Sometime in 1939, when cinemas were cinemas . . . it was afternoon . . . I was in the gallery. The film was romantic and there was no background music. Just silence heightened by the slight crackle of the sound equipment. On the screen were two large faces, his and hers, closing up for the exquisite surrender of the first kiss. From the depths down below came a child's voice, high-pitched and audible:

'I *ain't* picking my nose.'

Revd R. Grenville Clarke, Bury St Edmunds

Overheard on a bus in Reading. Two girls were sitting behind me and one said:

' 'E needn't have done that to me even if I was Beauty Queen last year.'

C. J. Norman, Goudhurst

On the top of a London bus years ago – but a fruitful source of conjecture ever since – a young woman was heard saying to her companion:

'Yes, my dear, just ordinary stewed pears, so they dug a hole . . . '

Mrs U. N. Weeks, Islip

Peter Cook, the humorist, claims to have heard one woman say to another:

'I think it would heal the rift – which has gone on too long – if Prince Charles made the gesture and married the Duchess of Windsor.'

I overheard a smart young man in a pin-striped suit say nonchalantly to his girlfriend as they drank coffee in a West End restaurant:

'It's about time we started giving some of your friends the illusion that we are having an affair.'

Olivia Rigby, Henley

On the tram not so long ago, I heard a woman talking to a friend about her old mother:

'Sie sitzt ganz still in der Ecke den ganzen Tag. Ich glaube Sie wird es kaum merken wenn sie stirbt.' ('She sits in the corner very quietly all day. I doubt whether she'll notice when she dies.')

Mrs Moya Frenz St Leger, Düsseldorf

Celia Haddon, the writer, overheard a sad tale from a woman on a bus:

'We came down in the morning and there he was at the bottom of his cage with his legs all blue. The vet says he must have had a heart attack.'

83

'The vet says he must have had
a heart attack.'

In his book *The Life of Noel Coward*, Cole Lesley recalls how the Master would contrive to get the same table every day in the restaurant at Raffles Hotel in Singapore to eavesdrop shamelessly on two American ladies. Among the pearls he gathered were, 'Ah, but then you would never wear that particular shade of blue. Your taste is so elite,' and:

'I found out what that white stuff was we had in Japan. It was rice.'

My late great aunt always used to promise us that she had heard one woman saying to another in a bus queue:

'Of course, he could always have borrowed my goldfish.'

Jenny Hartland, Leyburn

Walking with my family in Guernsey we passed two young men as one was telling the other:

'I had one up my trouser leg last year.'

Mrs Joyce Feasey, Bexley

Overheard in restaurant – elderly lady speaking to friend:

'Brenda says his big toenails go off like revolvers.'

Miss V. M. Smith, Croydon

WORD OF MOUTH

On the London Underground (Victoria Line), I heard one of those carrying, well-bred, female voices saying to her companion:

'I don't know about you, but as we get older I always find we get more and more like ourselves.'

Miss Bernice Hanison, Haywards Heath

Overheard in a bookshop:

'I shouldn't buy her that – it's all about what's going to happen in 1984, and as we're nearly there, it doesn't seem worth it, does it?'

Miss Renate Hornung, Bournemouth

Whilst walking through Stevenson Square, Manchester, in the early 1920s, I passed two navvies, one of whom was saying to the other:

'It's not the same warmed up.'

More than fifty years later I am still wondering what 'it' was.

Mrs C. Gould, Letchworth

Terence Frisby, the actor and writer of the long-running West End hit *There's a Girl in my Soup,* overheard a man talking about his fiancée:

'She's with the gas board and I'm an embalmer, so naturally we don't see a lot of each other.'

'his big toenails go off like revolvers.'

'She's with the gas board and
I'm an embalmer, so naturally
we don't see a lot of each other.'

The following conversation was overheard in a northern supermarket:

> *He:* **'I say, what was the name of the teabags them monkeys talked about on the telly.'**
> *She:* **'PG Tips.'**
> *He:* **'I think we should get some – they spoke very highly of them.'**

Mrs Joan Scott, Burton

When passing through Perkins' Rents in London, I heard a lady say in sinister tones to a small boy:

> **'You do that just once more, my lad, and I'll put jam behind your knees.'**

D. K. Womersley, Pulborough

Overheard in a large department store during the sales. Exasperated mother to small child:

> **'No, dear, the Queen is *not* the only person who wears gloves.'**

Mrs P. L. Roskrow, Chelmsford

Travelling some years ago on a Midland Red bus, two young women were talking earnestly. As they got up and made to get off, one girl was saying:

> **'Of course, the trouble with my mother is that she never had any children . . . '**

Mrs D. D. Pickering, Streetly

WORD OF MOUTH

A tourist visiting Windsor Castle was annoyed by the sound of aircraft taking off from Heathrow airport nearby and remarked:

'What a pity they built the castle so near to the airport.'

> *Traditional* (a variation of the even more traditional remark about the monks having built Tintern Abbey too close to the road).

In a Liverpool snack bar we overheard a voice just like Carol's in *The Liver Birds*, saying:

'If I 'ad a figure like 'ers, I'd walk on me 'ands.'

> *Margaret E. Roberts, Barnt Green*

Heard on the bridegroom's side in a fashionable London church where we sat collegiate style (facing across the aisle):

> *Lady in large hat:* **'It's astonishing how ordinary the other side looks –whichever side you are sitting on.'**

> *Comm R. S. Flynn, Fareham*

Some years ago my sister and I at a whist drive heard two ladies talking at an adjoining table. One said:

'Surely you must remember *her*? She ran off to London with a married man – and took the piano with her.'

> *James McCarten, Thornaby-on-Tees*

Old lady overheard in a village bus in Devon:

**'That there house is where the woman's
husband had a terrible brainwave and
died.'**

Miss G. Palmer, Hove

My favourite overheard conversational
snippet:

**'I haven't seen it since you ate that
trifle.'**

Miss J. Swift, London SE27

Plucked from the air by the poet and novelist
P. J. Kavanagh, this remark:

**'Mad, I don't say. Strange, I grant you.
Many's the time I've seen her nude at
the piano.'**

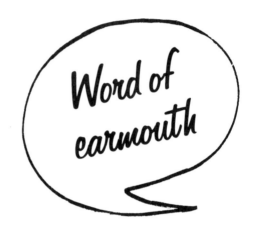

Overheard in a London store:

A: 'What can I get Harold for
Christmas?'
B: 'How about a nice book?'
A: 'He's got a book.'

Miss E. Kissan, Bournemouth

Overheard in a city store:

**'And if that wasn't enough, the little
swine stuck back the baby's ears with
Araldite.'**

Revd Andrew Macnab, Sutton Coldfield

While travelling on a train to Crewe, I
overheard two men talking. One said:

**'Mind you, I take my hat off to
prostitutes.'**

Bill Baker, Birmingham

Walking along a quiet suburban road recently,
I heard one elderly man say to another:

**'I'd have married her meself, only
Mavis Davis doesn't sound quite right,
do it?'**

Alison Young, Sheffield

As Phyllis Dixey, the stripper, entered a
restaurant in Plymouth with her husband,
Jack Tracey, I overheard one waitress say to
another:

**'If that's what she got for showing hers,
I think I'll keep mine covered.'**

Michael Finlay, Mytchett

We were travelling on a bus in Ireland when a
woman with a small boy took the seats directly
in front of us. Said the mum to the small boy:

**'Take your cap off, Patrick, so that the
wind can blow the dandruff from your
hair.'**

Lady Ingleby-Mackenzie, London SW7

An agitated lady came into the lost property department of a big West End store. She said that she had lost two children:

'I wouldn't mind, only they aren't mine.'

Mrs Linda Cover, London SW4

Overheard in a London coffee bar. A girl said to the man standing by her side:

'*Darling,* **did you know that your wife's boyfriend is a friend of my husband's girlfriend?'**

Clive Bright, Harpenden

I overheard this terrifying snippet of conversation in a north London pub:

'An' if there's one fing I can't stand, it's razor blades in me tea.'

Marilyn Bullen, London N10

Overheard on a bus to San Sebastian:

A: **'And what are your neighbours like?'**
B: **'Oh, quite normal. He's a French foot-juggler who's doing a summer season at Scarborough.'**

Mrs J. M. Balderston, Cleethorpes

Take your cap off, Patrick, so that the
wind can blow the dandruff from your hair.'

Picture a dingy, disorganised little greetings
card shop in Weston-Super-Mare, with a little
old lady saying to a bemused shop assistant:

**'Do you have anything for twenty-five
years at Marks and Spencers?'**

Chris Jeffree, Edinburgh

Heard on the Marine Parade at Brighton:

**'And, my dear, there was nothing in that
room but a great double bed. And there
was a framed text on the wall above it
which said** *He is coming.*'

Miss B. Saxon Snell, Henley-on-Thames

Overheard on top of a No. 2 bus, departing
from Swiss Cottage in a southerly direction:

**'There she lay, my dear, naked to the
navel, with Alfie's choc-ice melting on
her middle.'**

John Shearman, London NW3

Walking along Eltham Road, Lee, the day it
was announced that Montgomery had crossed
the Rhine:

First lady: **'Isn't that good news – Monty
has crossed the Rhine.'**
Second lady (in a rather doubtful voice):
**'Yes, but actually I wanted him to cross
much higher up.'**

Reg Spry, Chichester

Winn.

'...e's a French foot-juggler who's
...sing a summer season at Scarborough.'

Malcolm Bradbury, the novelist, admits – like most writers – to having at one time kept a notebook for jotting down stray remarks which could later be incorporated in his books. 'You go to parties', he says, 'and you slip off to the lavatory halfway through to start putting down all the things people have been saying during the course of the evening. I don't do it any more but I dug out a dusty old notebook which contained the following remarks gathered at parties':

> **'I feel so at home here . . . they've borrowed so many of our things . . . '**

And a man talking about teaching his wife to drive:

> **'I told her, if you can't stop the thing then run into something** *cheap.***'**

Here is something I overheard. A small crowd had gathered. They were looking at the top of a tall building. A man stood on the edge of the roof and was threatening to throw himself off. I joined the crowd and a woman next to me turned to another woman and said:

> **'If he doesn't hurry up I shall miss my bus.'**

Richard Whiteley, Huddersfield

Overheard on a train from Liverpool Street to Chelmsford, shortly after British Rail introduced the 24-hour clock in the timetable. One lady was bemoaning to another her inability to comprehend the hours after noon. Her friend replied:

'But my dear, it's quite easy. I have got a system. I just pretend they are pennies. Then, I convert them to shillings and pence and throw away the shilling.'

Bryan Carey, Chelmsford

Overheard by me when passing a group of well-dressed Third World persons in the lounge of a well-known Institute in London. One lady to another:

'But, of course, I'm not *me* any longer – I'm *we* . . .'

G. Black, Beverley

Holidaying in Donegal five years ago, we overheard this memorable exchange. A large Irish family trooped off the beach, heading towards the road – a long procession of parents, children, grannies, uncles, clutching inflatable beds, deckchairs and picnic baskets. To our surprise, they all plodded back about fifteen minutes later, still heavy laden, and as they passed us we heard the leading man say, in a heavy Irish voice:

'Now, tell Daddy *where* you buried the keys.'

Louise Ross, Leicester

'Now tell Daddy where you buried the keys.'

Overheard as two teenage girls passed by:

'I think lipstick looks dreadful on a horse.'

Mrs A. O'Neill, Ash

A friend of mine, now dead, overheard the following on top of a Clapham omnibus. Two middle-aged ladies were in conversation. One said to the other:

'I washed it for her when she was born, I washed it for her when she got married and if she thinks I'm going to wash it for her again she's got another think coming.'

Alison Elliman, Denham

When Pavlova gave her last performance in Edinburgh, the audience went mad with excitement at the end. They cheered, stamped, sobbed with emotion and flung flowers on the stage. Two ladies on the front row were clapping genteelly and one observed to the other:

'She's awfully like Mrs Wishart.'

Traditional

Overheard in a West End department store. Customer to assistant:

'I can't find the invisible thread.'

Mrs Sheila M. Carroll, Harlow

101

Old ladies leaving theatres are always being heard making inept comments on plays. Here for a change is one that is quite perceptive. First old lady, after seeing *Uncle Vanya:* 'Not much of a story was there, dear?' Her companion replied:

> **'No, dear. But I did feel at the end that we knew all those people so much better.'**

Overheard in a restaurant near Oxford:

> **'Of course, it's all right for Roman Catholics and Americans but it doesn't do for ordinary English people.'**

Tony Neale, Banbury

I overheard this in a hospital waiting room fifty years ago. Two elderly ladies were talking about the funeral of a friend who had died of an internal complaint. One said to the other:

> **'Wish I could have had her legs – she had a lovely pair of legs. Such a waste.'**

Mrs F. E. Straker, West Ewell

Overheard outside Bristol University –harassed father to importunate three-year-old daughter:

> **'Kindly understand, once and for all, that is *not* the zoo.'**

Miss D. M. Woodcock, Hewelsfield

Under our tents I'll play the
                              eavesdropper,
To hear if any mean to shrink
                              from me.

Shakespeare, *Richard III*

Overheard on top of a bus whilst passing a
crematorium in Edinburgh:

**'That's where my aunt's funeral was.
She wanted to be buried but she doesn't
know to this day that she's been
cremated.'**

Mary Boucher, Clitheroe

103

I was walking along the pavement one summer when three elderly ladies were approaching me deep in conversation. As I passed, I heard one say to the others:

'He was absolutely useless, you know. In fact, in the end I had to cut it off.'

G. W. Simpson, Bournemouth

Overheard conversation between two women:

'She's got trouble with her eye. Doctor says it's a misplaced rectum.'

Mrs Eileen Woodward, Halstead

This was on a No. 88 bus – a mini tourist trip round London. As we turned into Great Smith Street in Westminster one American tourist turned to another, thoughtfully, and said:

'I wonder who Great Smith was?'

Judy Lowe, London EC2

Two country women on the front seat of a double-decker bus running into Bishop's Stortford one Monday morning:

'Look dear, Chinese restaurant *(indicating newly-opened shop).* **You know, I wouldn't have thought there were all** *that* **many Chinese in Bishop's Stortford.'**

Pat Dalley, Hastingwood

The actress Denise Coffey overheard this telephone conversation:

A: **'I stood there till my vest was drenched but I never saw one.'**
B: **'I told you, rabbits can't climb up to hanging baskets.'**
A: **'Well, who's nibbled the nasturtiums, because they've definitely been nibbled. I know nibbling when I see it.'**
B: **'Perhaps it was a horse?'**
A: **'How would a horse get into the cemetery?'**
B: **'Yes, I see what you mean. It's a real problem.'**

My wife and I stopped for lunch at the White Hart Hotel at Nettlebed. An elderly lady was sitting, having lunch alone. She was obviously a well-known local person and was also deaf, for several people greeted her with their voices raised. A young man sat at an adjoining table and asked how she was. 'I'm well,' she replied, 'but I have had a sad blow – Laura died last week.' 'I'm so sorry to hear that,' said the young man, 'it must have been a great shock to you.' 'It was,' said the lady, 'she was nearly fifty you know.' The young man then said, 'Well, I don't think she did too badly on the whole.' To which the lady replied:

'No, she never got over the moult.'

W. G. Busbridge, Abingdon

'She never got over the moult.'

A royal eavesdropping – of which there is more than one version – concerns Queen Mary. During the First World War she was presenting medals to a regiment recently returned from the Front. Having pinned a medal on one soldier's tunic, she was moving on down the line when she overheard him say, 'No more bloody wars for me, mate.' To which the Queen, in her dignity, is said to have responded:

> **'No more bloody wars, no more bloody medals . . . '**

In his posthumously published autobiography *Ruling Passions,* Tom Driberg, the journalist and Labour MP, recalled travelling once on top of a bus from Tunbridge Wells to Crowborough. Two women behind him were talking about 'her'. One said, 'She was aways very kind . . . It was a shame what those soldiers did to her bees.'

The other added:

> **'They say she's been *seen* . . . quite often . . . in her black veil – at the end of the lawn, where they bees used to be.'**

They were talking about Driberg's late mother.

Whilst visiting hospital I overheard an elderly man say:

> **'I'm not afraid to die . . . dying isn't so bad . . . the trouble is that you're so bloody stiff the next day.'**

Jack Jennings, Hampton Bishop

'Dying isn't so bad ... the trouble is that you're so bloody stiff the next day.'

I was sitting in the Inter-City 125 at King's Cross waiting for it to depart for Newcastle when from the seat behind I heard an elderly male north-eastern voice address what subsequently transpired to be an Australian spinster with these words:

> **'You'll excuse me saying so but you've got a spot on your lip which is exactly the same as the spot which my wife had on her lip and which grew to enormous size ... before she died.'**

Brian Waters, Hexham

Overheard in the local post office:

> **'It's two years since I done it and I found mine has two little little red lights on.'**

L. James, London SE6

Rob Buckman, the doctor and humorist, was on a train going to Leeds when he overheard one old lady saying to another:

> **'I told him to take it seriously. I said, "Homosexuality is not something you can afford to turn your back on".'**

A woman sitting next to me in the cinema, watching Geronimo sneaking up on a US Cavalryman:

> **'Look out, Geraldo's behind you!'**

E. Lyons, London SE24

WORD OF MOUTH

This was overheard in a small Welsh village by a friend of mine. Two old ladies were discussing the death of the short-lived pope, John Paul I. Finishing the conversation, one said to the other:

'Well, it's his wife I feel sorry for.'

Nicola Wesson, Pontyberem

I can vouch for the following, which I overheard on a London bus. Behind me, two chirpy teenaged office girls were discussing the then new material Bri-Nylon.

A: **'I have a set of Bri-Nylon undies. They're very nice, but awfully pricey.'**
B: **'I have a Bri-Nylon nightie.'**
A: **'How lovely, I could never afford anything like that.'**
B: **'I didn't buy it. My sister gave it to me. She bought it for her honeymoon and never wore it.'**

F. D. Byers, Ipswich

I overheard the following conversation between two thin, elderly people sharing our table in the Covent Garden crush bar during a supper interval in a Wagner opera. She said, 'I'm not surprised the marriage hasn't lasted. He was so unreliable and he had such an unsteady job.' He said, 'I always thought he was something in Education.' And she said:

'No – he's a Judge.'

Tony Hepworth, Bradford

Heard by my wife in Victoria:

'You know my friend – the one who stuck the leeches on Humphrey Bogart for that film *The African Queen.***'**

Stephen Powell, London SE20

When foreign holidays were less common than they are nowadays, I overheard two young women on a bus discussing a third. One said to the other:

'She's an awfully nice girl – her parents are going to Yugoslavia for their holidays.'

E. Neale, Winchcombe

Patrick Garland, the theatre and TV director, says the most withering indictment he ever heard was of a well-meant but rather pretentious play at Brighton. He saw it at a matinée and as the curtain came down to rather desultory applause the woman in front of him turned to her neighbour and said:

'Well, Emily, all I can say is, I hope the dogs haven't been sick in the car.'

I overheard two ageing ladies talking in the queue at Marks and Spencers. One said:

'I always have to take a valium before I go to Sainsbury's . . . '

Shirley Jaffe, Little Gaddesden

Overheard at Warwick Castle – a lady American tourist while looking at a painting of Henry VIII:

'Doesn't he look just like the actor Keith Michell who was in that series on TV.'

T. J. Gill, Cheltenham

After the second interval at the opera when the conductor came to the rostrum to join the orchestra, the woman in front of me turned to her neighbour and said:

'He's always last.'

Mrs Manning, Helpston

I was sitting on a coach behind two American tourists. As we passed the Houses of Parliament, one asked what it was. The other replied:

'Well, I don't know, but it must be either Oxford or Cambridge.'

Sally Bigwood, Reading

Heard in Douglas:

'It was terrible. I couldn't see the mantelpiece. I was glad I had my hat on.'

Miss Audrey Kermode, Douglas

'I always have to take a valium
before I go to Sainsbury's.'

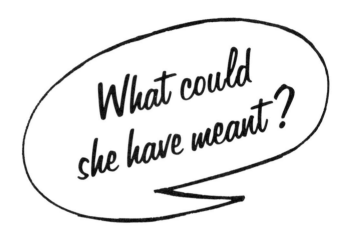

Overheard in the walled rose garden at Hampton Court – elderly lady to elderly gentleman:

'You see, dear, you can do *anything* **against a wall.'**

Mrs Annette Hynd, London W2

Overheard on a bus – I had to go on a further two stops to find out what it was all about:

'He does it very well considering he's only got one leg.'

Cricket was being discussed apparently.

Mrs Joan Lees, Moseley

I overheard this snatch of conversation in a coffee-shop restaurant. Two middle-aged women were at the table behind mine and one said:

'Of course, I've always wondered how Ethel managed without her kidneys. Doesn't seem natural somehow, but then she was always unlike other people, losing her things and never missing them.'

Janet Edwards, London SW10

Overheard on a bus, two women talking. One said:

'And they both agreed there was nothing worse than jam behind the brooch.'

Mrs J. W. Pinney, Stone

Overheard in a pub in Tottenham Court Road – the speakers looked like well-dressed young executives:

A: **'How did you get on?'**
B; **'OK, but I couldn't think what to do with the bits of marmalade.'**
A: **'Had you eaten them?'**
B: **'Yes, of course.'**
A: **'Well, leave it until you get to the end of the day then put it in a bag with the noodles. Mr Rothshaw will collect it.'**

Pauline Davies, Pevensey Bay

115

This was overheard when I cycled past a man and woman who were locked in a passionate embrace:

Man: '**Can I see you tomorrow?**'
Woman: '**Well, I'm gettin' married in the mornin' but I'll meet you here in the afternoon.**'

Bernard People, Andover

In the ladies' cloakroom at the Royal Academy of Music, I was in the loo when I overheard a very agitated girl's voice saying:

'**Don't pick it with a pin, Lynne.**'

Mrs Margaret Nockles, Epping

I was attending a London Symphony Orchestra Concert at the Royal Festival Hall. After an efficient rendering of Beethoven's Pastoral Symphony, the elderly American gentleman sitting in the seat next to me turned to his companion and earnestly confided:

'**Yeah, I sure liked the beat.**'

Valerie J. Percy, London N3

Two American tourists were heard going round Stonehenge. One said:

'**It hasn't changed much since we were last here five years ago.**'

Traditional

'Mr Rothshaw will collect it.'

117

Overheard on a tram in London before the war, as if it were the total explanation. One lady to her friend:

'Oh yes, she had the harp up on the bed with him.'

Ian Rodger, Brill

Heard on a bus in Croydon – two middle-aged ladies talking in the seat behind me:

'Well, if Myrtle has a bath every day, what does she want to buy black corsets for?'

Miss P. Simson, Mere

Overheard in a pub:

'I'm fine now. Ever since I bumped into my psychiatrist in the same ward as myself I have never looked back.'

J. R. Williams, Llandudno

Travelling on a train to Dorking, an elderly couple near to me were discussing either their neighbour or an acquaintance and the lady said:

'Oh, he's nice, he always speaks – through the dog, of course.'

J. M. Phillips, Horsham

Arthur Marshall, the writer and broadcaster, constantly has his ears cocked for curious remarks. Once on a bus he heard a beefy man declare:

'It was the first ball of the season – and I tonked it for six, clean over the pav!'

On another occasion, in Switzerland, he observed an enormous lady and her husband out skiing. The woman said, 'I'd love to go on a luge.' The husband commented, quietly:

'It'd have to be a huge luge . . . '

Overheard in a chintzy teashop:

'Such a nice gentleman, dear, and sells *delicious* apples, but of course I had been warned our auras would not mix.'

Two cockney women were chatting in the street and, as I passed, one whined, 'Naobody knaows what I suffers.' The other said briskly:

'Well, ducks, yer can't blame yerself fer that. Yer does yer best to tell us.'

Miss Nancy J. Quayle, Winchester

Walking one day in Oxford, I saw two elderly dons coming towards me engrossed apparently in some weighty discourse. As they passed me, I overheard just two words:

'And ninthly . . . '
S. H. Jarvis, Bristol

119

Ann Leslie, the journalist, overheard a bizarre remark on the telephone:

> 'So I said, "What do you want to nick a bollard for?" And he said, "It'd be a good gimmick to have the only bedroom in North Finchley which had an illuminated *Keep Left* sign in it".'

I overheard the following in Leicester Square Underground Station. One man to another:

> 'I had to tell her I couldn't do it that way. I just couldn't get at it.'

> *Brian Freeland, Nottingham*

Long ago on a tram – yes, a tram – near New Cross Gate, two local ladies passed me. One said to the other:

> 'Yes, she died, yer know. I've not seen 'ide or 'air of 'er since.'

> *Mrs I. Cochrane, Torquay*

Overheard at bus-stop. The speaker was a very thin lady, dressed in black, with one bandaged leg, addressing a man I took to be her husband:

> 'The Archdeacon always said you were a psychopath.'

> *Glynne Hughes, Liverpool 17*

'And ninthly...'

WORD OF MOUTH

I was sitting on top of a No. 29 bus which had stopped opposite the old Wood Green Town Hall on its way to Palmers Green in 1938–9. A cockney factory girl said to her friend:

'So I sez to 'im "Oh", and 'e sez "Oh, it's 'Oh' is it?" and I sez, "Yes, it is 'Oh'." '

This was a story often repeated over the years with varying intonations by my friend Dorothy Reynolds, the actress. Another favourite of hers was a Birmingham mother saying to her small son:

'Just look at your fingers! They're filthy! Suck 'em – go on – suck 'em.'

Mrs G. H. Alston, Lewes

Overheard at work:

'Oh, I do like my bidet! You don't have to have any blankets on the bed.'

Heather Pudner, Swansea

Some years ago, walking along Oxford Street, I overheard one lady say to another:

'She's worried about her little boy. He's had a lot of trouble with his back legs.'

J. Christian Salveson, Loughborough

On a cliff walk in South Devon, I stood back to allow a group of middle-aged-to-elderly hikers pass me. I overheard one lady with a very broad Devonshire accent say to her friend:

'The trouble is, when he goes on holiday his cucumber goes limp.'

Maureen Verdon, Romsey

Overheard in the Gare du Nord, spoken by a furious (very English) man:

'Je vous avoir savoir que je ne suis pas quelqu'un que vous trifler avec.'

Mrs Ivo Clark, Stirling

My husband and I were attending an antiques fair as exhibitors. I noticed two ladies approaching deep in conversation, paying no attention to the exhibits. As they passed our stand, one was heard to remark:

> **'And it wasn't until after he'd gone that I noticed the heap of sawdust on the sofa.'**

Norah Pearce, Wellington

I overheard the following segment of conversation between two ladies in a café:

> **'Her Mam used to take her to the school bus every morning and meet her off it again at night, but she still doesn't know how she got pregnant.'**

Nick Read, Leicester

Two old ladies outside a pet shop:

> **'I've never known anyone love dumb animals as she does – drowns all her kittens in warm water.'**

Mrs M. Pickering, St Helens

While browsing in a small branch library, I heard a very audible whisper on the other side of the bookshelves:

> **'I do not know why she left him. He had fitted carpet simply everywhere.'**

M. Heslop, Solihull

124

Je vous avoir savoir que je ne suis pas quelqu'un que vous trifler avec

Overheard at a jumble sale when I was standing behind the table of men's clothes – a mother and daughter after measuring a pair of trousers in great detail. The mother said:

'Well, this will fit two of his legs, anyway.'

Penny Slade, North Crawley

In Sheffield Park, Sussex, two ladies passed me by, one saying in a loud voice:

'And they dropped a box of bananas on it in West Wittering.'

Dr James J. O'Donnell, Brighton

During the blackout in the Second World War a voice was heard urging, 'Come on, Grandpa.' The old man explained he could not find his teeth. To which the reply was:

'They're dropping bombs not sandwiches.'

Traditional

We were standing on a terrace at Blenheim Palace admiring the view with many other tourists when a large American lady with an equally large voice declared:

'Isn't it beautiful? Of course, you know, it was designed by Capability Smith.'

Mary L. Perkins, Bournville

126

'He had fitted carpets simply everywhere.'

I overheard this while on holiday in Suffolk:

'My sister-in-law's marriage was never consummated, but I don't know the "ins and outs" of it.'

Elissa Munns, Gravesend

My late husband called into a pub on his way back from London. Sitting in the corner was a very small man wearing a cap and puffing away at his pipe and sagely nodding his head. His companion, a large very talkative character, was holding forth:

'She always was a big girl – big-chested, you know. But as I said to her Tuesday, "It might not be what you think it is at all, but all part and parcel of something quite different".'

Smudge Burnaby, Beckenham

Overheard across a crowded room:

'My dear, when you think of all the visits she paid to that clinic in Malta . . . and look where she is now.'

Ivy Willett, Bedhampton

128

Overheard in a dry cleaner's in Saffron
Walden:

**'He's a nice quiet boy. He comes to
practise his trombone at our house.'**

Janet Snart, Wendens Ambo

Arriving at the annual garden party of the local
Anglican church, a woman steered her aged
parent towards the welcoming vicar and said:

**'Oh, Father, you haven't met Mother,
have you?'**

Mrs E. Constable, London N20

Sir Malcolm Sargent used to recall how people
in concert audiences do not realise that
although a conductor may have his back to
them he can still overhear conversations in the
front rows. He once heard a lady say to her
friend:

'I wish my backside was as flat as his.'

Overheard in a SW1 café – a foreign
gentleman, well-versed in the English use of
euphemisms, asked a harassed waitress for
'the cloakroom'. She replied:

**'We 'aven't got one, you'll have to use
the 'atstand.'**

Mrs P. S., Eastbourne

winn.

'... you'll have to use the 'atstand.

I overheard two women chatting. One said:

'I had a week last week I can tell you. On Monday, our Ernie ended up in hospital with a broken collar-bone; on Tuesday, Auntie Ginnie collapsed and died at the bingo; and on Thursday, I won a bottle of sherry in the British Legion raffle. Isn't it funny how things always seem to happen in threes.'

D. E. Jones, London N2

Overheard at a deb dance in 1937, drawled as a couple rotated past:

'But it takes elephants *two years . . . '*

The Hon. Elizabeth Keyes, Tingewick

My favourite overheard remark on a crossed telephone line:

'What happens then? You hold it and I cough?'

Mrs Elizabeth Robinson, Penarth

Two women on a bus discussing their plants.

First woman: **'How come you know so much about plants?'**
Second woman: **'Well, when my husband died I buried myself in the garden.'**

Mrs Joan Cruse, London E6

WORD OF MOUTH

Two ladies were discussing the relative dampness of their flats. Said one:

'I've heard tell that some people have even got *mildred* on the wall.'

Vera Hughes, Bassett

During the war, standing in a queue at the local grocer's, a customer in front of me asked for some Marmite. When told that the grocer was still waiting for it to come in, the customer paused and said:

'Well, have you any brown boot polish?'

Mrs F. R. Chandler, Cliftonville

Overheard in Boots. One of two middle-aged women noticed a bottle of Minadex on a shelf and said:

'I bought a bottle of Minadex for my father the day before he died. I was told it was supposed to do you good. If I had known what would happen I would have bought the smaller size.'

Susan Fraser, Sheffield

Two typists overheard waiting for a lift. One was saying to the other:

'I'd take an onion rather than a kipper. An onion fits more easily in the pocket.'

Lynda Miles, Bridgnorth

. I buried myself in the garden. '

My husband and I often indulge in conversations in pubs and restaurants which are *intended* to be overheard – so this is, I suppose, a case of the biter bit. We were playing the game over a meal when the woman at the next table turned to her husband and said in a loud voice:

'By the way, dear, where did you leave the helicopter?'

Jane Meredith, Banbury

In Canterbury Cathedral two old ladies were gazing at the spot where Thomas à Becket met his death. As a friend of mine passed by he heard one lady say to the other, in a tone of patient resignation:

'No, dear, not *married – murdered.'*

Revd Michael Burgess, Broadstairs

Overheard whilst behind the immortal 'two ladies on a bus':

First lady: **'We went to Camber Sands on Saturday.'**
Second lady: **'Was it nice?'**
First lady: **'Well, there's miles of sand. In fact, they filmed parts of that Lawrence of Olivier there.'**

Chris Knipe, Reading

134

When in New Zealand some years ago, I went to look at the American space capsule which was being shown round the country. Two elderly ladies were in the queue in front of me. On looking at the cockpit, one of the ladies said, 'Oh, look, they have seat belts.' To which the other replied:

'Yes, dear. They're compulsory now you know.'

Neil Cooke, Market Drayton

During the bread strike I overheard this in a queue:

First woman: **'There was that French queen said, "If they can't get bread, let them eat cake."**
Second woman: (after deep thought): **'Ah, but it isn't everybody likes cake – my husband wouldn't look at it.'**

Mrs G. O'Connor, Darlington

On a seat in Basildon Town square, two women talking:

A: **'Did you ever get rid of the blancmange?'**
B: **'Yes – I told Dad he'd have to choose between it and me. He saw the sense and gave it to Oxfam.'**

Margaret Vincent, Basildon

135

'He saw the sense and gave it to Oxfam.'

While waiting to be served in a shoe shop I watched the woman in front of me trying some shoes on. She looked at them in the mirror, paused, then turned to the assistant saying:

'I like them, I'll take them both.'

Hilary Anne Farmer, West Linton

Overheard at the Royal Academy Summer Exhibition, where several large abstract paintings were being scrutinised by an elderly lady and her friend. One said to the other:

'They've put all the worst ones in one room.'

Wendy Davies, Solihull

I was in a queue at a large department store in Wolverhampton where Robert Dougall was signing copies of his book. The lady next to me, obviously very excited at seeing Robert Dougall in the flesh, was heard to say to her friend:

'It's *just* like him, isn't it?'

Margaret Bell, Cannock

On a local bus – lady to depressed friend: 'You *are* looking better. You've had your hair done.' The reply:

'Yes, but I really need a new lampshade.'

Mrs D. Hurford, Bristol

Overheard recently in a shop:

'Would this paper be suitable for a downstairs toilet?'

Mrs C. A. Hackett, Wellingborough

Overheard conversation during a bus ride. Lady to friend:

'A funeral is bad enough, but this one was terrible. To start with, the hearse was half an hour late, and then when it came it had L-plates.'

Mrs M. J. Pearson, Urmston

While I was watching an inter-college football match at Cambridge between Trinity Hall and Jesus College, one of the spectators was heard to shout:

'Come on Hall, you can nail Jesus!'

S. B. Jeffreys, Cambridge

At a football match between two primary school teams a parent was yelling encouragement to the Catholic schoolboys:

'Come on, Our Lady of Heaven, get stuck in!'

Lewis Howdle, London SW15

'... I really need a new lampshade.'

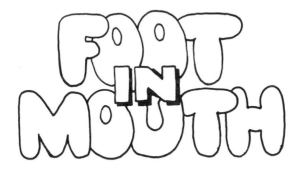

FOOT IN MOUTH is the umbrella title given to a whole range of verbal gaffes we delight in drawing attention to on the radio programme *Quote ... Unquote*. A 'foot in mouth' is not just a social clanger dropped in conversation. It can arise in one of those classic categories: Malapropisms, Spoonerisms, Goldwynisms or (more recently) Gielgudisms. Or it can occur as a notice or sign, in a note to teacher, over the air as a broadcasting 'boob', or as a misprint in a newspaper. A 'foot in mouth' is not just an error, however. Ideally, it is an inspired error.

I'll try and give you an example of what I mean. After we have recorded an edition of *Quote ... Unquote* – and we always record about ten minutes more material than we need so that the whole programme can be tightened up – the tape is transcribed. This makes the producer's job much easier during editing. The transcribers do not have a very enviable task as they try and render in sensible prose the ravings of sundry show-offs, all speaking at once. But their partial hearings can give rise to some very intriguing scripts. On one occasion when we had Terry Wogan as a guest he used the idiom, 'Groves of Academe'. To my delight, this emerged on the printed page as 'Groves of *Aberdeen*.'

On another show, when John Mortimer was telling an involved anecdote about Alfred Lunt and Lynn Fontanne, the famous theatrical couple came out as 'Alfred Lunt in Linford, Hants.'

MALAPROPISMS are, of course, named after the wonderful character 'Mrs Malaprop' in Sheridan's play *The Rivals* (1775) who has an unerring instinct for choosing the wrong word – 'headstrong as an allegory on the banks of the Nile', 'the very pineapple of politeness', and so on. Shakespeare and Smollet had seized upon this quite common human failing before him but it was Sheridan who named the complaint, employing the French phrase *mal à propos,* meaning 'inopportunely, inappropriately.' From the contents of this book you will be left in no doubt that Mrs Malaprop is alive and well wherever English is spoke. A bookseller in Leicester was asked, 'Have you got Thomas Hardy's *Tess of the Dormobiles?'* Further examples appear as **SCHOOLBOY HOWLERS**.

When we come to **SPOONERISMS**, named after the Revd William Spooner (1844-1930), Warden of New College, Oxford, who was given to transposing the beginnings of words, it is good to find so many of his fellow clergymen still maintaining the tradition – and being big enough to admit it. I am not qualified to say why it is that some people are particularly prone to this form of word-blindness. There is the story of the man who had drunk too much drink at lunch and was stopped by the police as he drove to his office. 'The main thing,' he thought hazily, 'is to be polite.' As the police officer bent down to look in the car, the driver flexed his face muscles and said, 'Good consternoon, affable'. But spoonerising can just as likely occur when you are not under the affluence of incohol.

Many of the Revd Spooner's most famous utterances are probably apocryphal though James Laver, the late fashion historian, once assured me he had heard from Spooner's own lips the phrase, 'Through a dark glassly...' One is tempted to ask: if Dr Spooner had been an ornithologist, would he have called himself a word-botcher? The point is, of course, that he did not just botch words, he did so delightfully. As did Ira Gershwin who once wrote a jolly song (to music by Kurt Weill) called 'The Cosy Nook Trio' which played pleasingly upon this form of verbal felicity. An Italian Duke, lusting after a painter's model, sings, 'I cannot promise bedding wells.' To which the model replies, 'My thoughts were not on wedding bells.' And neither were his, presumably.

Which brings us to the **FREUDIAN SLIP**, the **SOCIAL CLANGER** and the **DROPPED BRICK**. A Freudian slip is when by seeming to make a mere verbal error we give away our real intentions, as when a host offering to take a female guest's coat says, 'Can I take your clothes off?' I recall a delightful moment several years ago when watching a court-room scene in a musical at the Theatre Royal, Stratford East. The judge was addressing three leggy ladies who were the cause of much distraction in the court. But the actor playing the judge stumbled over his lines and declared roundly (corpsing the cast in the process), 'Stop clittering up the court!'

A number of years ago, an audience of tittering sixth formers (including myself) believed it had encoun-

WORD OF MOUTH

tered another example of this type. We were attending
what was known as a Film Appreciation Lecture in the
Philharmonic Hall, Liverpool. The speaker was a
distinguished director, whose name fortunately I have
forgotten, and he was introducing one of his
distinguished films. In a throwaway line, he informed
us he had just been with Dirk Bogarde in the South of
France or somewhere, 'And we've been disgusting
together ... er ... discussing ... oh God!'

To these traditional gaffe hunting grounds, the
preparation of this book has enabled me to add some
splendid examples of the printer's art – **MISPRINTS**
or 'literals' as they are known in the trade – and some
editorial usage of words which could have done with a
bit more sub-editing (but which, fortunately for us,
did not get). We do not use these on *Quote ...
Unquote* because they must be *seen* to be best appre-
ciated. But here they are now, in living black and white.

While enjoying what sometimes results from the
hectic compilation of printed matter, it is only fair to
put on the page some classic examples of
BROADCASTING BOOBS (which are known in the
US as **BLOOPERS**). Whether dating back to the
formal days of wireless (when the fall from grace was
so much further) or from the excessive ad-libbing
and informality of today, I felt it was time these magic
moments were preserved in a form other than
boot-leg recordings. I must apologise if any of the
attributions are wrong but I would not lightly pass up
some of these gems on a mere technicality.

My own favourite is from the former (and otherwise rather good) Radio 1 disc-jockey, Johnny Walker. Reading out a request he said the listener who had sent it lived in: 'Bury St., Edmunds, Suffolk.' And I really did hear an Irish radio announcer play a record on RTE for a listener who had been – remarkably Ill – a little while before:

'Oh, I'm sorry, he's been *ill* recently...'

If only one could recapture in print the full force of some other broadcasting boobs, like the time when William Hardcastle bounced on to *The World at One* and almost said, 'This is William Whitelaw...' Or found himself completely incapable of uttering the name 'Herbert Chitepo'.

Another of the Radio Greats in this sphere was Jack de Manio, one-time presenter of *Today*. His speciality was getting the time-checks wrong but I can still recall the *frisson* across the nation's breakfast tables when Jack was back-announcing an interview with a clergyman who had condemned wife-swapping in a parish magazine which just happened to be called 'Cockcrow'. What Jack said was:

'The Revd ——— on what Mr Fletcher MP calls 'our sex-ridden society. And I can't wait to get my cock... er... my copy of 'Cockcrow'!'

One of the most delicious radio boobs was not, alas, ever broadcast. A too-kind studio manager pointed out to the distinguished academic who was introducing a discussion on aspects of British

Industry that it would be better if he rephrased the words he had used at rehearsal. The academic had planned to introduce the speakers and give their credentials and fields of specialisation, thus:

'Michael Clapham – Director of ICI – chemicals; Val Duncan – Managing Director of Rio Tinto-Zinc – mining; R. D. Young – Deputy Chairman, Alfred Herbert – the Biggest Machine Tool in Europe.'

As with Spoonerisms, **GOLDWYNISMS** attributed to the Master himself are often, if not generally, apocryphal. As Samuel Goldwyn himself once declared, 'Goldwynisms! Don't talk to me about Goldwynisms. Talk to Jesse Lasky!' But the Polish-born film mogul's life-long struggle with the English language deserves a place in a book like this and I have tried to find some lesser-known examples. Incidentally, one wishes that one could have had James Thurber's presence of mind when arguing with Goldwyn over the amount of violence that had crept in to a film treatment of his story *The Secret Life of Walter Mitty*. 'I'm sorry you felt it was too bloody and thirsty,' said Goldwyn. 'Not only did I think so,' replied Thurber, 'I was horror and struck.'

Again, when it comes to **GIELGUDISMS**, one is faced with the question of authenticity. Sir John Gielgud, the great and good actor, is known throughout and beyond the theatrical profession for his dropped bricks. People find him all the more endearing because of this little peccadillo. Indeed, one gets the impression that half the actors in England are

hovering by Sir John, waiting for him to let one drop. I have included a tiny sample, one of which at least is absolutely genuine.

The accidental coming together of words is a basic element of humour. A *Quote . . . Unquote* listener told me of receiving a card on his wedding anniversary which the Post Office had franked with the slogan, 'NOT GETTING ON? Telephone the Marriage Guidance Council.' This was only capped by a colleague who had received a letter from the Race Relations Board franked with the slogan 'KEEP BRITAIN GREEN'.

Notices and signs seem to attract the 'foot in mouth' treatment, especially, as in the battle over lavatories in the House of Lords, following the introduction of women in 1958. The lavatories were originally labelled 'LIFE PEERESSES ONLY' but, as Lady Wootton pointed out, 'We are very passionate that we are not peeresses; peeresses are the wives of peers.' Now the lavatories are marked 'PEERS' and 'WOMEN PEERS'. And so on and so forth. I am most grateful to the numerous people who have contributed tongue-slips and fox's passes to this volume – especially to those who have foregone brain-wipe and admitted to verbal indiscretions of their own. I hope the experience has proved therapeutic. Where possible I have given credit. I apologise for any omissions.

As a writer and broadcaster who occasionally stumbles and who quite frequently commits appalling grammatical errors, I must emphasize that the purpose of this book is not to mock the perpetrators of the gaffes contained herein. I know what it is like to be mocked. Once in the dawn's early light when I was introducing the *Today* programme I ventured to suggest that 'Vanessa Redgrave had to run the gamut of protesters.' It took a mention in the *New Statesman* 'This English' column, a rebuke in a book on the declining standard of English usage, and a trip to the dictionary to make me realise what I had done.

What I hope the gaffes recorded here have in common, however, is not some terrible, ignorant, awfulness but a quality that transcends the grammatical, linguistic or social error upon which they are based – pick-me-ups, in fact, not put-downs.

Scottish Chamber Orchestra: Simon Rattle conducts a bizarre juxtaposition: the "Erotica" and Weill's *Seven Deadly Sins* (January 28, Queen's Hall, Edinburgh; January 29, Bonar Hall, Dundee; Jan 31, Theatre Royal, Glasgow).

● The Times

H erbert Marshall

was a British actor who made a name for himself in Hollywood during the 1930s despite losing a leg in World War I. He was between marriages when – or so the story has it – John Gielgud encountered him with the words:

'Ah, Herbert, I see you're foot-loose in Hollywood…'

Convent
of the
Sisters of Charity

NO PARKING
NO TURNING

Walk-out by 150 cripples top hospital

● *The Yorkshire Post*

Of her son,
taking his finals for an international job, a cousin
of mine said:

*'Of course, if he does well in them, the world's
his lobster.'*

She also said about her daughter-in-law who was
in hospital about to have a Caesarian baby:

*'Nothing to worry about. With a father who's a
top surgeon she's bound to get R.I.P. treatment.'*

A. M. D. CARRIER, LONDON SW7

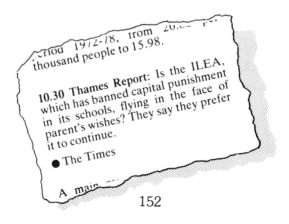

...riod 1972-78, from 20.0... ...
thousand people to 15.98.

10.30 Thames Report: Is the ILEA,
which has banned capital punishment
in its schools, flying in the face of
parent's wishes? They say they prefer
it to continue.

● The Times

A main...

At the Wimbledon Championships
Billie Jean King was seen to toss the ball in the air
and observe its movements. Dan Maskell helpfully
explained:

*'Billie Jean has always been conscious of wind
on the centre court.'*

Also at Wimbledon,
a BBC Radio commentator was waxing eloquent
about a South American player:

*'It's remarkable when you consider that in the
whole of Paraguay there are only about two
hundred tennis players. Victor Pecci is one
of those.'*

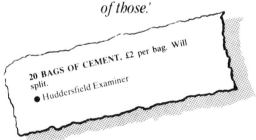

20 BAGS OF CEMENT, £2 per bag. Will
split.
● Huddersfield Examiner

153

On BBC news
from Norwich there was an item about an open
day at Wisbech sewage farm which included the
following passage:

*'A spokesman for the East Anglian Water
Authority said they considered a trip round the
sewage works a unique and interesting day
out. They were even laying on transport for
people who wanted to go.'*

THE HITE REPORT ON
MALE SEXUALITY
September
£12.50 (cased)
£9.95 (limp)

154

A lady
who used to come to help with the housework was
talking to my sister about her son's
forthcoming marriage:

*'His employers have been very good to him. As
he had no holiday time left they have granted
him passionate leave for his honeymoon.'*

MRS E. F. HOLMES, HOLLAND-ON-SEA

Garage, West Midlands

TOILETS

Quadruple stamps
for 4 gallons or over

155

Educated at Manchester Grammar School, he spoke English with a Lancashire accent, sold his father's German books, reduced the intake of German food and drink, and sent *his* son to Rugby and Roedean.

● Jewish Telegraph

"I know Sir Peter hasn't forgot-
t...

'And after the news
at 9 o'clock, you may like to know that there
will be a talk by Sir John MacPherson on "The
Land of the Nigger."'

JACK DE MANIO, BBC HOME SERVICE, 29 JANUARY 1956

'That's the end
of the forecast. Now here is the weather.'

RONALD FLETCHER, BBC RADIO

On a visit to Warsaw in December 1978, President Carter told the Poles: 'I have come to learn your opinions and understand your desires for the future.' The American interpreter translated this as:

'I desire the Poles carnally.'

In a reference to the President's departure from Washington, the translation came out:

'When I abandoned the United States, never to return...'

Carter's Press Secretary Jody Powell said: 'It was not a good translation. There will be a new translator tomorrow.'

which includes a light lunch.

Stockport Research Interest Group. Wednesday, January 28, 7pm, School of Nursing. Stepping Hill Hospital. Speaker, Anne Thompson: *Why don't women breast feed?* Cheese and wine party follows.

● The Nursing Times

WHATEVER the future may hold, it is currently an

Bristol flower group pick their leader

● The Bristol Evening Post

I went
to see an old lady and asked how she was:

*'Oh dear, I've 'ad an 'orrid shock. My neighbour
next door went to one of them parties last night
and fell down dead with a trombonis.'*

HELEN HIGGS, WIMBORNE

A t a luncheon given by Mervyn Hayt,
sometime Bishop of Coventry, a nervous curate
said to Cosmo Lang, Archbishop of Canterbury:

'Have another piece of Grace, your Cake.'

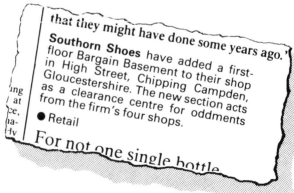

that they might have done some years ago.'

Southorn Shoes have added a first-floor Bargain Basement to their shop in High Street, Chipping Campden, Gloucestershire. The new section acts as a clearance centre for oddments from the firm's four shops.

● Retail

For not one single bottle

158

A married lady
was bemoaning to fellow dinner guests that she
had been extremely naive before her marriage.
To illustrate the extent of her innocence
she remarked:

*'I didn't even know what a homosexual was
until I met my husband.'*

MARY DRURY, PLYMOUTH

Sardine living in Osaka mini-hotel

● The Times

donations to Royal Opera House Development
Fund or the Royal Philharmonic Society.

**GARDEN PARTY – 2nd June,
2.00 – 5.00 p.m.**
The Rector of Buxted has
much pleasure in extending
to you
A Personal Invitation
on behalf of the P.C.C. of the
Parish Church of St. Margaret
the Queen. By kind permission
of Mr. & Mrs. Geoffrey Miskin
we invite you to attend a
Garden Party to be held in the
Grounds of Tanyards,
Framfield Road.
The Buxted and Warbleton
District Band will play a
selection of light music
throughout the afternoon.
Admission to the Garden
Party will be free but a charge
will be made for tea.
NB Bring an umbrella!
No toilet facilities provided.

**Police put tail on
'dognap' gang**

FOUND in telephone kiosk in Scarborough,
gent's trousers. –
● The Mercury, Scarborough

In the early days of radio,
a leading churchman was conducting a live
religious service, conscious that he had to
modulate his voice to make it more acceptable for
a studio than for a church. After he had concluded
the broadcast with the Grace, he commented to
the producer: 'I don't think that was too loud, do
you?' Unfortunately, this came over the air as:

*'... the fellowship of the Holy Ghost, be with us
all evermore... I don't think!'*

ble decker buses carried 420
children and their mum.

The Harrogate Council of
Churches are holding a series
of hunger lunches during
Lent at the Friends' Meeting
House, Queen Parade each
Friday afternoon. Come and
join them.
and unto dust thou shalt
return".
● The Harrogate Advertiser

Born Jerry Silbermann.

During the 1948 war
in Palestine, the US Ambassador to the United
Nations, Warren Austin, hoped that the Jews and
the Arabs would settle their differences:

'Like good Christians.'

At the wedding
of some friends of mine, instead of saying
'Lawfully joined together' the priest said:

'Joyfully loined together.'

BARBARA REEVE, CHELMSFORD

one of
page
ighton

al her

Road,
the
USA,
Tools

arner
nd a
idgid

s of

Mr Latham said: Before
he lectures working peo-
ple on wage claims, he
should look to the
Church's own affairs.
"In my constituency of
Paddington the Church
Commissioners are forc-
ing up rents by several
pounds per wee.

● The Paddington Mer-
cury

162

WORD OF MOUTH

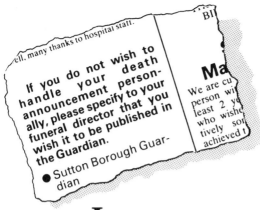

...ell, many thanks to hospital staff.

If you do not wish to handle your death announcement personally, please specify to your funeral director that you wish it to be published in the Guardian.

● Sutton Borough Guardian

I was in a play
— Lord Arthur Savile's Crime
– and had the line to say, 'Then you should not object to Mr Podgers seeing your palm.' At one performance it came out as:

'Then you should not object to Mr Palmers seeing your podge.'

MISS M. F. DAMESICK, MANCHESTER

SHOP ASSISTANT REQUIRED.

NO OBJECTION TO SEX.

Looe

Trim labour saving home in relaxed environment, on gentle slopes above Willow Wood and Misbourne. Good value at **£49,500** for 988 years of peaceful enjoyment.

● Bucks Examiner

A WOMAN terrorist who has been held in maximum security prisons for nearly two ~~years is expecting a baby~~

A former headmaster
of Llandovery College said the following in a
prayer during morning assembly many years ago:

*'Bless us in our intercourse, be it for business
or pleasure.'*

JOHN JENKINS, LLANDOVERY

LUCKY VICTIM
WAS STABBED
THREE TIMES

● Hackney Gazette

164

WORD OF MOUTH

My mother was notoriously bad at remembering names. One year at a seaside boarding house Father suggested she should memorise some everyday word which rhymed with the name she wanted to remember. For a lady whose name was Crummock, Father suggested 'stomach'. Next day as this dignified lady entered the dining room, Mother paused a moment for thought and then chirped happily:

'Good morning, Mrs Kelly!'

SYLVIA TORKINGTON, STOCKPORT

Top men suffer

Of this year's tournament winners, Barnes suffered most of all, but Mark James and Vincente Fernandez were not far behind with their 77s, while one man, Des Smyth, walked in when he hit a wedge shot into the 13th and lost his balls.

● The Daily Telegraph

Patients cut to ease crowding

● Bristol Evening Post

Defender's broken leg hits Haverhill

● Cambridge Evening News

My elderly
aunt told me she had been to see the play:

'Arsenal and Old lace'

MRS A. ALEXANDER, NEWCASTLE-UPON-TYNE

'**M**r Thorpe insisted
*that he hadn't known Andrew Newton before he
went to goal, hadn't seen him while he was in
goal, and had had no contact with him since
being released from goal.'*

ITN REPORTER

nave done some years ago.'

After the Hungarian uprising of
1956, Kocsis moved to Switzerland
and layed for Young Fellows. Subsequently, he signed for Barcelona.
● The Daily Telegraph

The mixed saunas will be held
two days a week.

Cit⌁ ⌁⌁uncil ⌁⌁⌁der ⌁⌁ ⌁⌁⌁ Ken

Dan Maskell was providing
the commentary for TV coverage of a Braniff
Airways Mens Doubles tennis match in which
David Lloyd and Mark Cox were participating. At
one point he remarked:

*'The British boys are now adopting the
attacking position — Cox up.'*

WORD OF MOUTH

BBC2

3.10 SATURDAY CINEMA: 'THE SHOP THAT DIED OF SHAME' (bw) starring Richard Attenborough and George Baker.

3.00 THE SHOTGUN INHERITANCE. Seven films on present-day Japan and its debt to the past (2) 'Cherry Blossom and the Sword'

● The Town Crier, Cambridge

The old tea-clipper *Cutty Sark*
was being installed for public inspection in a
dry dock beside the River Thames at Greenwich.
In front of Prince Philip, sundry other
distinguished guests and the serried ranks of the
media, the Mayor of Greenwich proudly referred
to the vessel as:

'The Sutty Cark.'

move right in to back him up."

"The little children are more utgoing than the adults. They have all made genuine friends here and we have had no problems at all – well, only one. The smallest weer not used to wearing knickers.

● The Daily Telegraph

Mr Sid Weighell, general secretary of

169

WORD OF MOUTH

My favourite spoonerism
was alleged to have been originated by the Station
Commander at an RAF station in the Canal Zone
round about 1952 when I was there. At church
parade the order was given:

'Roam out the fallen Catholics!'

JACK EVANS, WIMBORNE

I collected my Grandmother
(aged 78) from a Christmas party where everyone
had supplied a dish. She got in the car and
announced that her stomach was giving her jip.
When asked why, she replied:

'Well, dear, I had chicken in Harpic.'

GILLIAN PARKER, MOULTON

Three fall down hole in shop

Three people were taken to hospital
yesterday after a 12ft hole opened up
under them in the Quick Turnover
Fruiterers in Gillingham High Street,
Kent.

● The Sunday Express

... by cyclists and roller skaters and people were using the lavatories as public conveniences.

New screwing method cuts fatigue and increases productivity

● Maintenance Engineering

CHARITY workers are combatting vandalism at a Hove church hall with a live-in warden. Last year a glass door was smashed, fire ... floors were damaged ...

TWENTY GOLDEN GOLDWYNISMS

1 'We can get
all the Indians we need at the reservoir.'

2 'Too caustic?
To hell with the cost, we'll make the picture
anyway.'

3 'It's spreading like wildflowers!'

4 'I want
you to make a bust of my wife's hands.'

5 'I read part
of the book right the way through.'

6 'You ought to take
the bull between the teeth.'

7 'Anyone who goes
to a psychiatrist needs to have his head
examined.'

8 'I'll give you a definite maybe.'

9 'First you have a good story, then a good treatment, and next a first-rate director. After that you hire a competent cast and even then you have only the mucus of a good picture.'

10 'Let's have some new cliches.'

11 'This makes me so sore, it gets my dandruff up.'

12 'The A-Bomb – that's dynamite!'

13 'Lets bring it up to date with some snappy nineteenth century dialogue.'

14 'I'd like to propose a toast to Marshall Field Montgomery Ward.'

WORD OF MOUTH

15 'Tell me, how did you love the picture?'

16 'I don't remember where I got this new Picasso. In Paris, I think. Somewhere over there on the Left Wing.'

17 'That's my Toujours Lautrec.'

18 'You just don't realise what life is all about until you have found yourself lying on the brink of a great abscess.'

19 'This is written in blank werse.'

20 'I want you to be sure and see my Hans Christian Anderson. It's full of charmth and warmth.'

Due to injury, the part of an Executioner will be played by Malcolm Ranson
● Manchester Royal Exchange Theatre

It happened soon after
the last war when many civilians were still wearing
Utility Clothing. My husband had to change trains
at Basingstoke and went into the Tea Room for a
cup of tea. A couple entered. The man was
wearing an almost identical hat and coat and
carried a very similar week-end case to my
husband's. They sat at the next table. The man
opened his newspaper and the woman went to the
tea counter. A few minutes later the woman put the
tray of tea and biscuits on the table and whispered
into my husband's ear:

*'Shan't be long, darling. I'm just going to
the doings.'*

HILDA F. READ, BARKING

WORD OF MOUTH

Heard in the sermon
at a marriage – the priest holy, innocent and
slightly dotty, said:

*'Sometimes in a marriage, the couple have
been known to get on top of each other...'*

REVD. B. PAUL GILROY, EWLOE

Sea body identified two years later

A MAN whose body was found in the sea at Penarth has been identified – almost two years later.

His niece said today: "He loved Wales very much and had visited the area many times in years gone by. He was a believer in euthenasia and the fact that he went back to Wales had something to do with that."

Blaze closes crematorium

BUSINESS at a crematorium chapel came to a halt on Monday when the premises were ravaged by fire.

● Wimbledon and Morden Guardian

WORD OF MOUTH

During a disagreeable discussion
on dogs, my mother-in-law made the following
observation:

*'Well, I think some dogs ought to be
compulsorily castrated. They shouldn't be
allowed to increase willy-nilly.'*

P. BRANTLEY, HARLINGTON

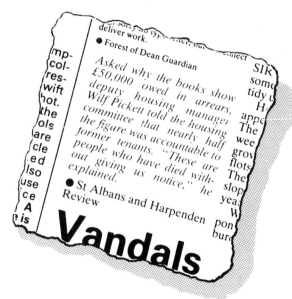

deliver work.

● Forest of Dean Guardian

Asked why the books show
£50,000 owed in arrears,
deputy housing manager
Wilf Pickett told the housing
committee that nearly half
the figure was accountable to
former tenants. "These are
people who have died without giving us notice," he
explained.

● St Albans and Harpenden
Review

Vandals

Young boy in Regent's Park:

'What's that funny building, Nan?'

Nan:

'It's where the Government sends foreigners to say their prayers. It's called a kiosk.'

RITA CANAVAN, SOUTHEND-ON-SEA

First Female Relative:
'When I was on holiday in Spain, I nearly got stung by those huge jellyfish.'

Second Female Relative:
'You mean the Portuguese Menopause?'

R. N. W. ELLIS, LLANGAMMACH WELLS

Gone are the days of senior boys flogging their juniors, while **capital** punishment by staff is undertaken to a much lesser degree than previously.
● The Stafford Newsletter

TERRORIST PREGNANT IN JAIL

A WOMAN terrorist who has been held in maximum security prisons for nearly two years is expecting a baby on March 18.

Embarrassed public prosecutors were yesterday carrying out an investigation, but 28-year-old Signorina Francesca Bellere is refusing to disclose the father's identity.

The justice ministry has demanded a full report. "This sort of thing makes nonsense of our claims that Italy's maximum security prisons are impregnable," said an official.

CARDINAL O FIAICH told the Catholic should play a leading role in the ecu

over the River Kennett is not completed soon, they fear there will be traffic chaos.

Slippery fish make jam on A2

If you don't have at least one dress gay number at Jane Thomson with daring slits at the sides you aren't Morningside Road, Church in the fash: Discovered a madly Edinburgh Dare one whisper

STROKE PATIENTS DON'T FEEL ALONE

Doctor's waiting room, Colchester

During the riots in Chicago during the 1968 Democratic Convention, Mayor Richard J. Daley addressed the press:

'Gentlemen, get the thing straight once and for all.
The policeman isn't there to create disorder, the policeman is there to preserve disorder.'

Joint body plan for cemetery

● The Hereford Times

181

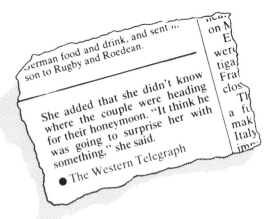

German food and drink, and sent ...
son to Rugby and Roedean.

She added that she didn't know
where the couple were heading
for their honeymoon. "It think he
was going to surprise her with
something," she said.

● The Western Telegraph

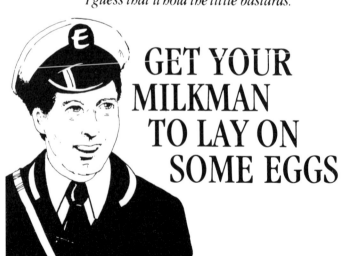

From 1928 to 1949,
'Uncle Don' – Don Carney – was the host of a
popular children's show on radio station WOR,
broadcast over a large part of the United States. He
spent his life trying to deny that he had ever let slip
one of the most famous clangers of all when,
thinking he was off the air, he said:

'I guess that'll hold the little bastards.'

GET YOUR MILKMAN TO LAY ON SOME EGGS

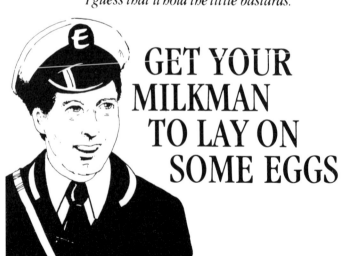

'**D**ear Miss, Sorry Jimmy is late
but me and my husband rather overdone it this
morning.'

'**D**ear Miss, Please excuse Mary
from having a shower, being how she is. Being
how you are yourself sometimes, you will
understand how she is.'

Top-hated
Bishop stole the
show at fete

● The Salisbury Journal

WORD OF MOUTH

'**P**rincess Margaret, wearing an off-the-hat face…'

MAX ROBERTSON, BBC RADIO

'**F**loods
of molten lager, flowing down the
mountainside.'

STUART HIBBERD, BBC RADIO

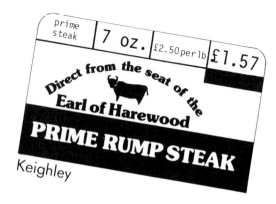

184

During the 1979 Cricket World Cup when England was playing Canada, BBC radio commentator Christopher Martin-Jenkins drew attention to the inclement conditions under which the match was being played:

'It is extremely cold here. The England fielders are keeping their hands in their pockets between balls.'

At the 1980 Democratic Party Convention in New York, prior to his ignominious defeat by Ronald Reagan in the Presidential Election, Jimmy Carter accepted his party's renomination as candidate by referring to some of the great Democrats who had never made it to the White House. In particular he mentioned:

'The Great President who might have been – Hubert Horatio Hornblower.'

$\mathbf{A}$ dear old great aunt
of mine died when I was about thirteen. The
grown-ups were discussing her – how she had
been a patient little woman with a bullying
husband. One was so carried away she
announced:

*'There's no doubt about it, he prolonged the
shortening of her days.'*

MRS C. E. MARTIN, NEW ROMNEY

AT
SHAFTESBURY TOWN HALL (GUILDHALL)
ON:–

Tuesday 11th. July at 8 p.m. Come and see:

–"The Final Hour" followed by tea & buscuits.

DR Ian Cross, 26, of Wood Lane, Ferryhill, made a brief visit to his parents, Joseph and Phyllis Cross this week. He had just completed one year at Gorum Gorum, Upper Travolta, West Africa, the only doctor in 80 square miles.

● Durham Advertiser

Asked why the books show £50,000 owed in arrears, deputy housing manager Wilf Pickett told the housing committee that nearly half

A WOM... held in max nearly two on March 1

Embarra were yester tigation, b Francesca close the fa

The jus a full rep makes no Italy's ma impregnab

● The Daily

BOOSEY. – O Hampshire, Ethel Torfrid

Many years ago
the then Lord Altrincham came to the local
Grammar school at Chipping Sodbury to present
the prizes. In the introductory speech, a local
councillor began:

*'How pleased we are that Our Lord has come
down...'*

MRS D. J. BROCK, BRISTOL

with gold insets of nude women, and it is about eight inches wide at the wildest point.

TOILETS ARE NOT NECESSARY

Ladies who like a flutter at the bookies won't be able to spend a penny – for bookmakers don't have to provide toilet facilities of any kind.

This was revealed to members of Dumbarton District Licensing Board.

At the previous meeting members were told that a gents toilet was available but no ladies loo – and they had heard rumblings from female customers.

● Helensburgh Advertiser

RANSOME. – 'To LORRAINE and Mervyn. God's gift of a son, on August 13th.

2.4
ible e
blow
explo
darin
the U

7.0
perfo
this
to Bl
tion
play)

My 'chat show —by the reggae riot Pc

SID SCOTT made his stage debut at a reggae concert … and stopped a riot.

As 'souffles' broke out in the huge crowd, he told the fans:

'This is nothing to do with you or the police. It's just an unfortunate incident.

● The Daily Star

A GREEK urn worth £200 was stolen from St Osyth Priory on Tues-

high, with two purple handles edged in gold.

Largest ever heroine haul

● The Newcastle Journal

A WOMAN held in max nearly two on March 18

'**A**t Oxford Crown Court today,
Donald Neilsen denied being the Pink Panther.'

EDWARD COLE, RADIO 4

I am a Lay Reader.
When taking evensong soon after my licencing I
called on the congregation to:

'Come with me unto the Groan of Thrace.'

BRYAN OWEN, DEAL

Vandals are kept at bay

CHARITY workers are combatting vandalism at a Hove church hall with a live-in warden.

Last year a glass door was smashed, fire extinguishers were let off, floors were damaged by cyclists and roller skaters and people were using the lavatories as public conveniences.

● Brighton and Hove Leader

Traffic will hit homes if motorway is scrapped

● The Sutton Hera[ld]

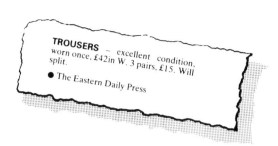

TROUSERS – excellent condition, worn once, £42in W. 3 pairs, £15. Will split.

● The Eastern Daily Press

A while ago, a friend of mine, who is a policeman, had occasion to stop a car and speak to its driver. The driver did not take kindly to being held up in this way and was being rather abrupt and unhelpful. His wife, who was in the car with him, felt obliged to try and calm down the situation before her husband got himself into trouble, so she leaned over and said to the policeman:

'Please don't pay too much heed to him. He's always like this when he's had a few.'

ALISTAIR EDWARDS, WILSMLOW

Geisha Night Club

At the 12th floor overlooking a Magnificent, Scintillating view of Cairo by Night is the "GEISHA" A Dance Band and an Oriental Dancer creating an Atmosphere of "A Thousand and one Nights" dont miss it . . ,

Take the Elevator and Press the 12th Bottom
NOW !

For your Diner we sugest . . .

"l'Entrecote GEISHA"

● Atlas Hotel, Cairo

EVERY time I switch on David Attenborough's TV programme "Life on Earth" I am faced with animals or reptiles copulating. Is the man sex mad?

(Miss) JEAN COX, Bicester,

● Daily Mirror

My wife and I were setting off on our honeymoon late in the evening, and an aged relative, on hearing that we had quite a distance to travel, inquired:

'Are you going all the way tonight?'

MATTHEW COCHRANE, MAGHULL

193

Redundant musicians

Ten musicians from the Western Orchestral Society – incorporating the **Bournemouth Sympathy Orchestra** and Bournemouth Sinfonietta – are to lose their jobs.

● The Daily Telegraph

KING'S College Choir School, Cambridge

Sir John Gielgud was being interviewed late at night on a local television show in St Louis, Missouri. Peter Ustinov, who just happened to be there watching it go out, recalls how Sir John was asked who had been the greatest influence on his early career. Sir John replied:

'Claude Rains. But I don't know what happened to him afterwards. I think he failed and went to America.'

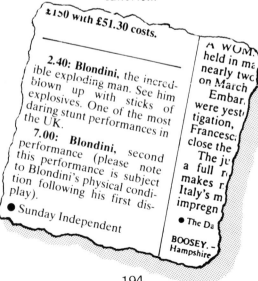

£150 with £51.30 costs.

2.40: Blondini, the incredible exploding man. See him blown up with sticks of explosives. One of the most daring stunt performances in the UK.

7.00: Blondini, second performance (please note this performance is subject to Blondini's physical condition following his first display).

● Sunday Independent

A WOM. held in ma nearly two on March Embar. were yest tigation, Francesca close the The ju a full r makes r Italy's m impregn

● The Da

BOOSEY. – Hampshire

194

David Smith, chief superintendent of Kensington New Pools in London said: "We could put chlorine in vast quantities into water and apart from bleaching your heir, it would have no effect.

● The Guardian

Embarrassed public prosecutors were yesterday carrying out an investigation, but 28-year-old Signorina Fra...

Sir John told the theatre director Patrick Garland that he was going down to Chichester to do a play with Robin Phillips whom he did not know. 'I hear he's very young,' commented Sir John. 'I know him very well,' replied Garland. 'He's about my age.' To which the Gielgudism was:

'Oh, he's not so young then.'

broken leg

CARDINAL O FIAICH told the Catholic clergy yesterday that they should play a leading role in the ecumenical movement and he made three suggestions as to how they could play out that role. He suggested that in offering prayers for persons recently deceased they include prayers for members of the local Protestant community who had died. He further suggested that Protestants be included in the priests' prayers for the sick.

● Cork Examiner

Worried Ousden residents are praying for
bridge over troubled waters. If work on

We were passing through the village
where Gray's *Elegy* was written when a lady at the
rear of the bus remarked to her companion:

'I have always wanted to go to Poke Stoges.'

NANCY REDFERN, CAMBRIDGE

'People behind
*Martina Navratilova on the roller, have the best
view of her receiving service.'*

MAX ROBERTSON, BBC RADIO

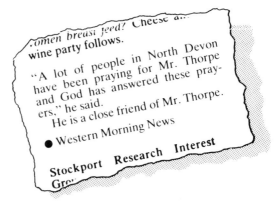

...omen breast feed? Cheese a...
wine party follows.

"A lot of people in North Devon
have been praying for Mr. Thorpe
and God has answered these prayers," he said.
   He is a close friend of Mr. Thorpe.

● Western Morning News

Stockport Research Interest
Gro...

h Interest
January 28,
rsing. Step-
Speaker,
Why don't
Born Jerry Silbermann, Wilder popped up

An artificial ski slope at Kidsgrove,
near Stoke on Trent was closed
yesterday – because of snow and ice.
● The Daily Telegraph

in the la
gay numb
Morningsi
Edinburgl

$\mathbf{A}$mple,

rosy-faced lady with bulging shopping bag on bus:

*'Yerse, she took up wiv one of them
new-fangled religions. You know, the Seven Day
Adventuresses.'*

CONSTANCE DARG, TONBRIDGE

$\mathbf{A}$t a Labour

committee meeting in the Midlands, the
Chairman, in his opening remarks, was heard
to say:

*'Brothers, as you all know, certain allegations
have been made against me. I will reply to these
at the next meeting after I have confronted the
alligators.'*

ERIC A. BIRCH, ILFORD

197

THIS IS THE BRITISH BROADCORPING CASTRATION

Golden Moments from the Wireless – the perpetrators of which remain, happily, anonymous:

"There is the danger of civil war if the Kurds don't get their way."

"A series of strikes at the Liverpool Royal Hospital has caused a lot of ill feeling."

"There is a trough of low pleasure over Europe."

"We are now to hear some Birdsong by Plain."

"Police fired rubber bullocks... er, sorry, bullets."

❝Widespread fist and mog can be expected.❞

❝There will be no sun
today because of an industrial dispute.❞

❝And now a record dedication
for Mrs Ethel Smith who is one hundred
years old today. But I'm told she's dead
with-it.❞

❝Aristotle Onassis,
the Greek shitting typoon.❞

❝We shall now hear Bolero's Ravel.❞

❝The trouble has been caused by
unpatriotic elephants in the country.❞

❝In winter bullfinches
are best fed on bacon rinds and great tits
like coconuts.❞

WORD OF MOUTH

❝More about that delay
on British Rail Southern Region. We have
our reporter on the line...❞

❝As a result of the strike
by Aer Lingus staff, anyone wishing to fly to
Birmingham will have to go by boat.❞

❝There has been a heavy fall of rain
here at Trent Bridge but fortunately it didn't
touch the ground.❞

❝And now we have
the Bathroom Orchestra from Pump.❞

❝The unorganised conference... er,
I'm sorry, the U.N. organised conference...❞

❝Reports are coming in
from Australia that Serbo Croat extremists
have attempted to sabotage the Sydney
water supply by *blowing* up the *pipes*.❞

2.00 After Noon Plus: Can the
Isishness of the Irish de defined ?
● The Times

$\mathbf{A}$nd
two bloopers from American radio:

*'We'll be right back after this word from
General Fools.'*

*'This portion of <u>Woman on the Run</u> is brought
to you by Phillips' Milk of Magnesia.'*

PLEASE DO NOT
LOCK THE DOOR
AS WE HAVE
LOST THE KEY

hotel Ireland

'**T**here's Neil Harvey
at leg slip with his legs wide apart, waiting for
a tickle.'

BRIAN JOHNSTON, BBC RADIO

This was only topped
by Brian Johnston commentating on the Oval Test
against the West Indies in 1976 with Michael
Holding bowling to Peter Willey:

'The bowler's Holding, the batsman's Willey.'

In Nottingham, travel agents believe the
threats will result in few cancellations of holidays.
    Mr. Tony Whittall, manager at Fairville
Travel in Clumber Street, commented: "It's
going on every day in Belfast. I don't think
bombs have the same sort of 'feel' about them
that they might have done some years ago."

● Nottingham Evening Post

Lorry driver John Hey Mellor was found guilty of carless driving and was fined £150 with £51.30 costs.

● The Yorkshire Evening Post

On another occasion Trevor Bailey had been singing the praises of Peter Willey when he suddenly produced this remarkable admission:

'I am, of course, a great Willey supporter.'

Brothers fell foul of law

TWO Ballygawley brothers fell foul of the law when they were caught by the police for two motoring offences.

They were Dennis Gillespie, an 18-year-old chicken catcher, and his 25-year-old brother, George, a hen catcher.

● Stabone Weekly News

At a conference in Berlin
in 1954, the French Foreign Minister, Georges
Bidault, was hailed as:

'That fine little French tiger, Georges Bidet.'

At one time a certain pop star
was famous for splitting his pants during
performances. An elderly lady with whom I
worked burst into the office and said breathlessly:

*'Did you hear about J. B. Priestley splitting his
trousers on stage?'*

MRS C. WHEELER, LONDON E.3

ENGAGEMENTS
MR. E. A. AUSTIN
MISS L. A. MORRIS

● Alton Herald

On a wet day
on holiday in France we borrowed a Scrabble set
from a French family. Later at a cocktail party in
England I was explaining to two friends how
difficult it is playing in English with two many QU's
and C's etc. In one of those terrible lulls in
conversation my voice rang across the room:

*'You've no idea how tiresome it is trying to play
Scrabble with French letters.'*

TONY ROUNSEFELL, CHELTENHAM

Gierek political eclipse

Mr Edward Gierek, the former Polish Communist Party leader, and
seven of his closet associates resigned
their parliamentary seats, completing
their political eclipse.

● The Times
The justice ministry has demanded
a full report. "This sort of thing

Oxford City Council is to press the Thames Water Authority to help improve sanity facilities along the river banks running through the city.

● The Oxford Times

'**M**iss Stove
seems to have gone off the boil.'

PETER WEST, BBC RADIO

Peter West – again – talking
about the seeding of Jimmy Connors
at Wimbledon:

'Connors' wife is expecting a baby and there
was some doubt about his entry.'

been
s for
baby

SINGER 367 sewing machine, never
used in anger, £75 ono.
● Evening Times, Glasgow

A WO
held in
nearly
on Mar

● **CATHERINE LA PORTE COOLEN**, talks to Gene Wilder in "Superstar Profile," (STV 10.30).

Born Jerry Silbermann, Wilder popped up in a small part in "Bonnie and Clyde" in 1967 and has been in a stream of funny, sometimes freaky, comedies ever since … from "Willy Wanka and the Chocolate Factory" to "The Adventures of Sherlock Holmes's Smarter Brother."

● The Evening Times, Glasgow

Mr
som
ome
. It
an
ne
st

P
'd

Su
mo
an
wo
so
bc
£3
lio
chi

fa

Biles succeeds Bum, promises to open offense

● Dallas Morning News

WORD OF MOUTH

My dear Norwegian mother
spoke quite fluent English but occasionally
became a little confused over proverbs. Her best
effort, I think, was when she reprimanded me for
being ungrateful about a present I had received:

*'Never, never, cast your teeth in a
gift-horse's face!'*

MRS E. S. B. PASHLEY, COTTINGHAM

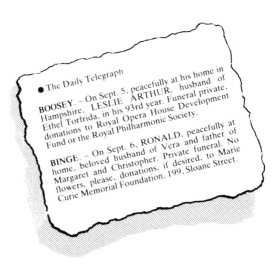

WORD OF MOUTH

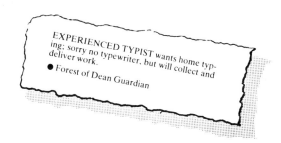

EXPERIENCED TYPIST wants home typ-
ing; sorry no typewriter, but will collect and
deliver work.
● Forest of Dean Guardian

President Richard M. Nixon once said:

*'Scrubbing floors and emptying bedpans has as
much dignity as the Presidency.'*

President Gerald R. Ford declared:

*'Whenever I can I always watch the Detroit
Tigers on radio.'*

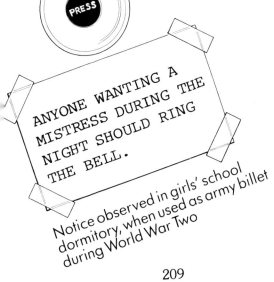

ANYONE WANTING A
MISTRESS DURING THE
NIGHT SHOULD RING
THE BELL.

Notice observed in girls' school
dormitory, when used as army billet
during World War Two

I had entered the wrong time in my diary for a Harvest Festival Supper at my church and consequently arrived an hour late. Wanting to apologise in a light-hearted way, I heard myself say:

'Ladies and gentlemen, I cannot remember ever being late for such a function as a Harvest Supper before, but it seems that tonight I have well and truly clotted my bottybook ...'

REVD JOHN E. BOURNE, STROUD

For not one single bottle gets the Löwenbräu label until the brew has been tasted and passed by a panel of German beer experts. Who have rigidly Teutonic standards when it comes to beer. (Amongst other things).

An Asian teacher nicknamed "Mr Wortical" who was sacked from a primary school because his spoken English and grammar were said to be below standard had been adjudged "not goon enough to teach in primary schools" before he took the post, it was revealed yesterday.

● The Daily Telegraph

A crony at work
told me a friend of his was up before the bench:

*'For living on the immortal earnings of
his wife.'*

JOHN TAYLOR, NOTTINGHAM

'The time
is twenty-half and a five minutes past eight.'

TOM CROWE, RADIO 3

impregnable," said an official...

And coloured workers are good trade unionists too. When the London bus strike took place, not a single coloured worker was a blackleg.

● Bristol Evening Post

were yesterday carrying out an investigation but 28-year-old Signorina to die.

"Superstar Profile,"

Fiona draws them in

SEX queen Fiona Richmond had promised to auction her knickers to raise cash for the children, but she had to let them down on the day.

● The Mercury

SAUCIER

ng
at
e,
a-
ly

We a
perso
least
who
tively
achie

● Th

Children-for-sale row

By OUR ATHENS CORRESPONDENT

A FURTHER inquiry into a couple on the Aegean island of Lesbos who have been producing children for sale to wealthy childless couples, has been ordered following protests from Greek women's lib organisations.

The protests are on the grounds that the mother is "the victim of the most extreme form of male exploration."

● The Daily Telegraph

While our scripture teacher
was telling us the story of one of the miracles, my
friend was surreptitiously toasting her toes on the
radiator. The teacher said:

*'Jesus walked on the water — and that, Jean
Morrison, is just the way to get chilblains.'*

MAUREEN THRELFALL, PRESTON

In Australia there is a deadly insect
called a Funnel Web spider. A newscaster is
reported to have announced:

*'This afternoon in Sydney a woman was bitten
on the funnel by a finger-web spider.'*

Bridgnorth Athletic Club has
folded because of lack of support by
athletes.

Mr Stuart Williams, who had been
running the club single-handed, said:
"There is a complete lack of apathy
in Bridgnorth. I am very sad about
what has happened."

● Bridgnorth Journal

My mother
was having a cataract operation and the lady in the
next bed told her that she was suffering from a:

'Detached retinue.'

JANE BAKER, THAME

Ed Stewart was introducing records
on his Radio 2 show and had been asked to play a
romantic record for an old lady celebrating her
89th birthday. He said:

'It's entitled, "Until it's time for you to go."'

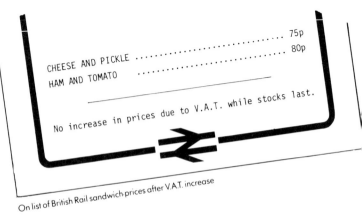

CHEESE AND PICKLE 75p
HAM AND TOMATO 80p

No increase in prices due to V.A.T. while stocks last.

On list of British Rail sandwich-prices after V.A.T. increase

Quiet village

The village of Lingdale was quiet today after the annual exodus to Scarborough on the outing arranged by the village working men's club. Eleven double decker buses carried 420 children and their mum.

● Middlesborough Evening Gazette

"The little children are more utgoing than the adults. They have all made

one. The smallest weer not used to wearing knickers.

The new South African Ambassador to Uruguay, Mr F. J. Fourie, told his first press conference in Montivideo, in May 1981:

'I am very happy to be in Peru.'

Jack de Manio was interviewing a newly appointed woman assistant governor at a man's prison. He asked her:

'Do you think the prisoners will regard you as a good screw?'

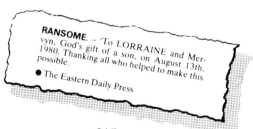

RANSOME. – 'To LORRAINE and Mervyn, God's gift of a son, on August 13th, 1980. Thanking all who helped to make this possible.

● The Eastern Daily Press

215

BRIGHTON'S Jane Warner is one of the country's top models, a page three pin-up, former Miss Brighton and magazine cover girl.

But this week we can reveal her latest title.

Miss Warner, 19, of Ryde Road, Brighton, has been chosen by the Ridge Tool company of Ohio, USA, to be their Miss Ridgid Tools 1979/80.

As winner of the title, Miss Warner got a free trip to America and a special bonus – a gold plated Ridgid Tool.

It was one of the little perks of my job."

● Brighton and Hove Gazette and Herald

Ap

SIR –
someon
tidy up

Here
appear
The r
weeds,
grown,
flotsam
The c
sloppy
year to
Wha
pondsn
bureau

● The

Pregnant woman acquitted

A PREGNANT woman was acquitted by the Nicosia District Court yesterday for violating the weekend motoring regulations by using her car to see her doctor.

Defence counsel Mr Michalakis Papapetrou told the court that the accused, Erini Eleftheriadou, of Pallouriotissa, was in the last month of her pregnancy and she went on Sunday to consult Dr Angelis at his clinic. Counsel presented to the court a certificate from Dr Angelis verifying the visit.

The court acquitted her under the reservation that she does not repeat the offence within nine months.

● Cyprus Mail

identified

WORD OF MOUTH

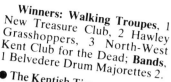

son to Rugby and Roedean.

Winners: Walking Troupes, 1 New Treasure Club, 2 Hawley Grasshoppers, 3 North-West Kent Club for the Dead; **Bands**, 1 Belvedere Drum Majorettes 2.

● The Kentish Times

TERRORIST

Shortly after the engagement
had been announced between Prince Charles and
Lady Diana Spencer, the Prince attended a
luncheon of industrialists and civic heads in
Glasgow. Mr Peter Balfour, a leading Scottish
businessman, no doubt conversant with the
names of many girls previously associated with
the Prince, proposed a toast wishing him long life
and conjugal happiness with:

'... Lady Jane.'

rina
dis-

nded
thing
that

FULL LENGTH undertakers coat,
left shoulder slightly worn, £6 —

● The Chester Observer

A bibulous guest at a Foreign Office
reception waltzed up to another guest and trilled,
'Lovely creature in scarlet – dance with me!'
The object of this request replied:

*'I am the Apostolic delegate and I don't think
you're in any condition to dance with me.'*

Angela Rippon in a BBC Television
news broadcast referred to a Government decision
to draw up:

'Gay puide-lines.'

Are your cook's drawers really good enough?

JUST go into the kitchen and make a swift check of the cook's drawers. Are they really the sort of thing you want around your food while it is being prepared? Can you remove them easily? Could you wash them, or even wipe them clean without a lot of frustration?

WHATEVER the future may hold, it is currently an electrical world. Those who have not yet switched on to it should sign up for one of the illuminating courses run by the Electrical Association for Women at its London headquarters. They cost £3, which includes a light lunch.

● The Guardian

Educated at Manchester Grammar School, he spoke English with a
L...

When it was discovered
that the Stone of Scone had been taken from
under the Coronation Chair in Westminster Abbey
(Scottish nationalists were responsible), the news
was handed to Lionel Marson as he read the Six
O'Clock bulletin on 25 December 1950. He
concluded the item by saying:

*'The Stone of Scone was first brought to
England in 1297 by Edward Isst.'*

When subsequently challenged, he replied that as
the news had been handed to him while he was on
the air, he had not had a chance to think about it.
'I realise now, of course, that I should have said
Edward Iced.'

My schoolteacher niece in New Zealand
gave her class of ten-year-olds a list of words
which were to be used, one at a time, in a short
passage to demonstrate their exact meaning. One
word was 'Frugal' which one boy clearly knew had
something to do with saving. He wrote:

*'A beautiful princess was at the top of a tall
tower. She saw a handsome prince riding by.
"Frugal me, frugal me," cried the beautiful
princess. So the handsome prince climbed the
tall tower and he frugalled her and they lived
happily ever after.'*

CHRISTINE BURDEKIN, TRURO

daring stunt performances in the UK.

Don't kill yourself in your garden Let us do it for you

● Yellow Advertiser, Basildon

Noel Coward

took part in a television interview on his 70th birthday. Admitting to a lack of formal education he said:

'I learnt all I know at Twickenham Public Lavatory... er... Library.'

A commentator on the

400 metres heats at the 1976 Olympic Games in Montreal asserted:

'Juantorena opens wide his legs and shows his class.'

...thing with my member, I wi... move right in to back him up."

The birth rate has declined, in the period 1972-78, from 20.82 per thousand people to 15.98.
A main cause of all this is the difficulty of making ends meet.
● The Observer

Are your

Youth triumph

GREAT BRITAIN and Ireland achieved a comprehensive victory over Europe, winning four of the five foursomes and eleven of the ten singles in yesterday's youth international golf championship at Woodhall Spa.

● The Daily Mail

One of the classic broadcasting boobs was committed by Macdonald Hobley, the BBC Television announcer, introducing a live Party Political Broadcast (indeed, probably the first of its kind anywhere in the world) in 1949. Seated in Studio A at Alexandra Palace with one of the leading politicians of the day by his side, he said:

'Here to speak on behalf of the Labour Party is Sir Stifford Crapps.....'

not good enough and something must be done about it."

─────────

SIR PETER PARKER

"I know Sir Peter hasn't forgotten me. I remember him at the dancing class as a girl of 14.

● London Evening Standard

TWENTY CHOICE
SCHOOLBOY HOWLER

1 'Pompeii was destroyed
by an overflow of saliva from the Vatican.'

2 'And Sir Francis Drake said:
"Let the Armada wait. My bowels can't."'

3 'Lot's wife
was a pillar of salt by day... but a ball of
fire by night.'

4 'The Black of Hole of Calcutta
was when two hundred English soldiers
were locked up in a tiny room with a little
widow with a very small hole... and in the
morning most of them were dead.'

5 'Queen Elizabeth
knitted Sir Walter Raleigh on the deck.'

6 'When Mary heard she was to be the mother of Jesus, she went off and sang the *Magna Carta*.'

7 'Our Lady and all the angels have lilos over their heads.'

8 'Christopher Columbus circumcised the world with forty foot clippers.'

9 'A kangaroo keeps its baby in the porch.'

10 'Last weekend, the Bishop came to our school and turned some of the Sisters into Mothers in a short, but interesting, ceremony.'

11 'The Romans did not conquer Whales because they did not understand what the welsh were saying.'

12 'Henry VIII always had difficulty getting Catherine of Aragon pregnant.'

13 'Henry VIII's wives – Chattering of Argon, Amber Lin, Jane Saymore, Ann of Cloves, Catherine Purr.'

14 'The Pope was inflammable.'

15 'Viking ships could sail up rivers because they had hoars.'

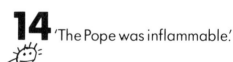

16 'Suffragettes were things the Germans shot under water to kill the British in the First World War.'

17 'I know that my reindeer liveth.'

18 'A cuckoo is a bird which lays other birds' eggs in its own nest, and *viva voce*.'

19 'An orchestra has a man called a conductor who stands out in front with a piece of paper which tells him what music the orchestra is playing.'

20 'Macbeth's courage failed him at the last minuet.'

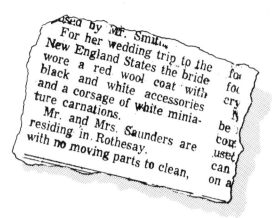

...sed by Mr. Smith.
For her wedding trip to the
New England States the bride
wore a red wool coat with
black and white accessories
and a corsage of white minia-
ture carnations.
Mr. and Mrs. Saunders are
residing in Rothesay.
with no moving parts to clean,

I was a District Nursing Sister
and was attending a parents 'do' at my son's
school. A strange gentleman came across to me
through the crowd greeting me like an old friend,
saying, 'You remember me, you came when I was
out of hospital with a fractured leg.' Light dawned
and I replied rather loudly during a lull in
the hubbub:

*'Oh, of course I know you. I'm so sorry, I would
only know you in bed.'*

RUTH GALE, HINCKLEY

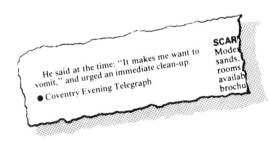

He said at the time: "It makes me want to
vomit," and urged an immediate clean-up.
● Coventry Evening Telegraph

SCAR...
Mode...
sands,
rooms
availab...
brochu...

228

In a coffee shop one morning, my mother and I heard a piercing female voice (belonging to my doctor's wife) cut through the gentle murmur, 'Every time I go into the garden I take off ten years.' This was followed by an embarrassing little silence filled by my mother's remark:

'She ought to stay out there.'

SUZANNE WILLIAMSON, BEXHILL-ON-SEA

Mr Charles Vaggers, once Mr Thorpe's staunchest political ally and his local chairman until last March, said: "There is relief and euphoria today, and the red carpet will be rolled out if Mr Thorpe comes to Barnstaple. But questions remain in people's minds. A lot of queer things have been happening."

● The Sunday Express

The event was a nativity play
and the Angel Gabriel announced his presence to
the Virgin Mary with the words:

'Hail! Thou that art highly-flavoured…'

ANGELA HOYLE, HALIFAX

'**A** *passing policeman*
was unable to revive Mr X despite using the kiss
of death.'

ROBIN HOLMES, RADIO 4

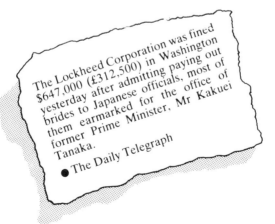

The Lockheed Corporation was fined $647,000 (£312,500) in Washington yesterday after admitting paying out brides to Japanese officials, most of them earmarked for the office of former Prime Minister, Mr Kakuei Tanaka.

● The Daily Telegraph

230

Our concierge will be happy to supply you with stamps, post-cards and any information you may require.We would ask you to contact the concierge immediately if you should have any problem regarding the hotel and its services, so that we are able to do all possible to give you complete satisfaction, and make stay a happy one.
Please don't wait last minutes then it will be too late to arrange any inconveniences.

● Hotel Caravel, Sorrento

WORD OF MOUTH

11.00 Frank Muir goes into Pubic-Transport.
● The Daily Telegraph.

The actor Peter Jones had just started to appear in the TV series 'Mr Big' when he was accosted by a lady in the street:

'Oh, Mr Jones, I do so enjoy your programme. It's so <u>mediocre</u> – something in it for the whole family.'

David Coleman described Asa Hartford, the footballer at one time thought to have a hole in the heart, as:

'A whole-hearted player.'

SYNOPSIS

ACT ONE

A small pizza in Venice

It is the day of the Duke of Urbino's masked ball and his valet tells the café-owner, Pappacoda, that his master wants to meet Barbara again – the masked girl whom he met last year.

● Theatre programme, Manchester

Notes on the

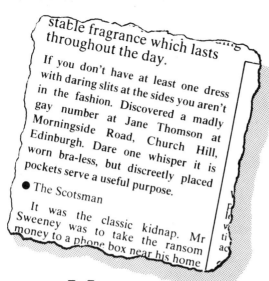

stable fragrance which lasts throughout the day.

If you don't have at least one dress with daring slits at the sides you aren't in the fashion. Discovered a madly gay number at Jane Thomson at Morningside Road, Church Hill, Edinburgh. Dare one whisper it is worn bra-less, but discreetly placed pockets serve a useful purpose.

● The Scotsman

It was the classic kidnap. Mr Sweeney was to take the ransom money to a phone box near his home

WORD OF MOUTH

My husband is a Minister much prone to gaffes. When a guest at a wedding reception told him that Mr So-and-So was in hospital for an operation on his piles, my husband commented:

'Poor man, he has had a rough passage this year.'

MRS J. EVANS, BRADFORD

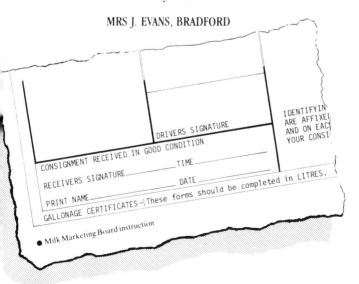

DRIVERS SIGNATURE

IDENTIFYIN ARE AFFIXE AND ON EAC YOUR CONSI

CONSIGNMENT RECEIVED IN GOOD CONDITION

RECEIVERS SIGNATURE_____TIME_____

PRINT NAME_____DATE_____

GALLONAGE CERTIFICATES—These forms should be completed in LITRES.

● Milk Marketing Board instruction

Rising costs hit jewellers balls

● Retail Jeweller

CARDINAL O FIAICH told the Catholic clergy yeste~ ~that they
should play a leading role in the ecumenical ~~~~~ ~~~ and he

LEAMINGTON-based Automotive Products, the vehicle component manufacturers, are on target for a record-breaking year in the export market.

"We have never been more optimistic about our future," said managing director Mr George Pears.

"We are now seeing the benefits of our long-term strategy to develop well-balanced business and diversify into new mistakes," he said.

● Birmingham Evening Mail

From the BBC 2 commentary on a doubles game at Wimbledon, 1980:

'He doesn't miss many like that, Brian Gottfried. He practises assiduously. He's the only married man on court.'

Received directly, face-to-face, in conversation with a friend some years ago:

'Ah, poor soul, she's got something eternal, you know. She's got a cyst on her aviary.'

DOROTHY MAIR, BRIGHTON

WORD OF MOUTH

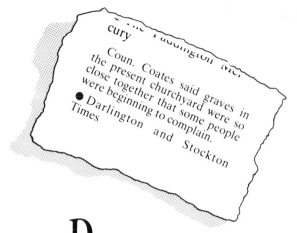

Coun. Coates said graves in the present churchyard were so close together that some people were beginning to complain.

● Darlington and Stockton Times

During World War Two
King Haakon of Norway was in exile in London
and from time to time made broadcasts to his
people over the BBC. On one occasion he is
reported to have arrived by mistake at Bush House
instead of Broadcasting House and approached
the commissionaire who was not, of course,
primed for his arrival. 'I am the King of Norway,'
he said and the commissionaire busied himself on
the telephone trying to find someone in authority
to sort out the muddle. At one point he broke off
and said,

*'Er, 'scuse me, but where did you say you was
King of?'*

Roast Turkey breast served
with gooseberry sauce and
stuffing.............................£4.65
Roast Lion of Pork with apple
sauce and stuffing...........£4.65
**Poached Local Salmon (as
available)**.......................£5.25
Roast Pheasant with cran-
berry sauce (as avail-
able..................................£5.50

● Evening Gazette,
Middlesbrough

I was taking a wedding for a couple. The groom had often said he was not going to come to church, he didn't want all that fuss. I opened:

'Dearly beloved brethren, we are gathered here in the sight of God and the fear of this congregation...'

REVD IAN C. HAWKINS, FAVERSHAM

A BBC foreign correspondent reporting the 1973 October War in the Middle East referred to the possibility of:

'Lesbian forces moving down from the North towards Israel.'

8.25 FREE TO CHOOSE. The case for free enterprise is examined by Prof Milton Shulman in the first of six programmes.
● The Daily Express

thousand peop

10.30 Thames I which has bann in its schools,

BLACKWELL. At Princess Mary
Maternity Hospital, on July 31, to
Malcolm and Norma (nee Watson) a
daughter, Nichola Jane, almost wel-
come sister for Christopher, a
grandchild for Mrs. E. Watson, sixth
grandchild for Mr. and Mrs C.
Blackwell. Mother and baby both
well, many thanks to hospital staff.
● Evening Chronicle, Tyneside

Quiet village

One of our WRVS members
asked an old lady if there was anything she
wanted. She replied:

*'Yes, I'd like a long-sleeved Cardinal to keep
me warm.'*

MRS J. M. THOMASSEN, BEXHILL-ON-SEA

David Bellan,
presenting *Starsound* on Radio 2, said *à propos* a
record request:

*'I hope you're listening, Bernard, as your wife
tells me that 'Calamity Jane' will bring back
memories of your honeymoon.'*

A high spot of next week's Festival music programme will be David
Pountney's new production of Tchaikovsky's masterpiece "Eugene
Onegin." John McKay's rehearsal photograph shows John Shirley
as Quirk in the title role.

● Glasgow Herald

238

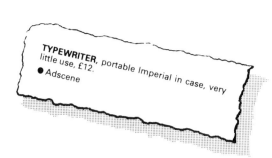

As a young girl
I was introduced by a friend at a party to a
formidable (to me – terrifying) uncle of his.
Proud at least to have remembered his name I said
ingratiatingly, 'How do you do, Mr Todd.' A
moment's awful silence ensued. Then my
friend said:

'Actually, it's Sweeney.'

KATHLEEN NEWELL, CHIGWELL

WORD OF MOUTH

'**D**ear Miss,
*Please excuse Sandra being late. She was
waiting for the bus at twenty to nine but came
back to use the toilet and missed it.'*

'**D**ear Miss Jones,
*Sorry Alan was away last week but with all the wet
weather he's had diarrhoea through a hole in
his shoe.'*

Scottish fishing strike collapses

SCOTTISH kippers admitted defeat as their three-week fishing
strike collapsed at the week-end.
● The Daily Telegraph

● jewellers balls

into

BELL OUT OF USE

PLEASE USE KNOCKERS

To mark his sixtieth birthday, Prince Philip gave a radio interview in which he said:

'A few years ago everybody was saying we must have much more leisure, everybody is working too much. Now that everybody has got so much leisure — it may be involuntary, but they have got it — they are complaining they are unemployed. People do not seem to be able to make up their mind what they want, do they?'

WINDSOR CINEMA

ENDLESS LOVE
CANCELLED
Due to technical problems.

● South Wales Evening News

241

Arthur Calvert, beagle of the
York Gild of Freemen
● Yorkshire Post

When I was working
in a canteen one of the staff said:

*'You know why we are rushed off our feet?
Because they keep giving them those
luncheon vultures.'*

MRS J. GRIST, HAMPTON

The remote beauty spots of
Epping Forest are well known
haunts for sex pests.
Numbers of sex crimes, indecent exposures to youngsters
and peeing Toms were so high
during the latter part of the '70s
that police repeatedly warned
people to take care in the Forest.

● West Essex Gazette
and Independent

FOR SALE recently acquired 2 second hand coffins, previous owner moving to warmer climate.

A local Mrs Malaprop spoke endlessly of her husband who suffered a lot with his 'slipped Dick'. She had been on holiday in a Carraway Van, the only complaint being that there was only one Emanuel Saucepan provided.

GERALD V. HALL, BATH

Wrong note!

Sir, – Thank you for including the article regarding my appointment as manager of the Twickenham branch of the National Westminster Bank on the retirement of Mr. Tom Bligh.

However, I would like to put the record straight in that my previous experience that my "18 months with a foreign bank," not "18 years with a foreign band", as stated in your paper.

● Twickenham and Hampton Times

WORD OF MOUTH

Three new members (including me)
of a well-known women's club had been asked by
the President to take coffee with her and be put at
our ease. We were indeed. She said:

*'Don't think the President is very special. Next
year I'll be nothing again, like you.'*

MARY PARKINS, NEW BARNET

I was in the company
of an elderly lady recently and there was some
argument as to the whereabouts of her airman son
at the end of the last war. Finally, to settle the
matter, she said:

*'Well, I know he was home on leave in May 1945
as we gave him a V.D. party.'*

KATHLEEN RICHARDSON, UXBRIDGE

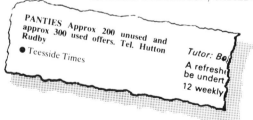

PANTIES Approx 200 unused and
approx 300 used offers. Tel. Hutton
Rudby
● Teesside Times

Tutor: Bo
A refresh
be undert
12 weekly

My dear old mother
and I were discussing a friend who had just left his
wife for a later model. She said:

*'I think it's disgusting. Where would he be
without her? Do you remember when he was
doing that PhD? She used to do all his typing –
and she used to sit up all night helping
him with his faeces.'*

BILL DUFFIELD, BANBURY

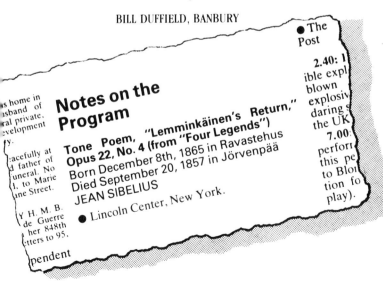

● The Post

2.40: 1
ible expl
blown
explosiv
daring s
the UK

7.00:
perforr
this pe
to Blo
tion fo
play).

s home in
sband of
al private.
evelopment
y.

acefully at
d father of
uneral. No
, to Marie
ne Street.

Notes on the Program

Tone Poem, "Lemminkäinen's Return,"
Opus 22, No. 4 (from "Four Legends")
Born December 8th, 1865 in Ravastehus
Died September 20, 1857 in Jörvenpää
JEAN SIBELIUS

● Lincoln Center, New York.

Y H. M. B.
de Guerre
her 848th
tters to 95,

pendent

111   1

Double Force

Velcro fastening

A show and a festival

The Royal Albert Hall stages, as always, the **Festival of Remembrance:** BBC1 (9.15 pm), and Radio 2 (8.30 pm) will be there. On Sunday the Cenotaph ceremony, including the two minutes' silence, can be seen on BBC1 and heard on Radio 4 (10.33 am).

8.2
An Evening in Vienna
Direct from the
Spa Grand Hall, Scarborough

9.2 *Stereo*
Among Your Souvenirs
with Walter Midgley
accompanied at the piano by
Gladys Midgley, Lissa Gray,
Harold Blackburn Balladiers, Clacton-on-Sea
Co-Operative Band
and the Reginald Leopold
Orchestra
Introduced by Alan Keith
Producer ROBERT BOWMAN

9.5 *Stereo*
This Week's Composer
Palestrina
Mass: Assumpta est Maria
CHOIR OF ST JOHN'S COLLEGE,
CAMBRIDGE
conducted by THE COMPOSER

● Radio Times

Sir John Gielgud was lunching with the actress Athene Seyler and fell to bemoaning his lot. 'I spend all my time in the company of these old bags of stage and screen – Monday, Fay Compton, Tuesday, Sybil Thorndike, Wednesday, Athene Seyler.' Then, realising what she might be thinking, he quickly added:

'Of course, I don't mean you, Athene!'

Police put tail on 'dognap' gang

It was the classic kidnap. Mr Sweeney was to take the ransom money to a phone box near his home and leave it inside a directory. It would be picked up later. The ransom fitted easily inside the phone book, for it was no great sum – just £35. And Mr Sweeney was no millionaire grieving over a snatched child.

The hostage was the Sweeney family's pet dog Rufus.

The following morning Rufus, a three-year-old pointer, was found tied to a railing near his home.

Said a police spokesman: "We are following certain leads.

● The Sunday Express

We were sorry to hear of the death of Miss Naomi Whelpton, a former Chichester Diocesan Moral Welfare Secretary (she was Mrs Shirley Emerson's predecessor). Miss Whelpton was trained at Josephine Butler House, Liverpool, and spent much of her time in this Diocese under Bishop Bell.

Jack Valenti, President of the Motion Picture Association of America, was being interviewed on the radio about the pressures under which the United States President has to operate. He said:

'People nowadays want him to be knowledgeable about every tit and jottle of all sorts of subjects.'

WORD OF MOUTH

SCARBOROUGH. Majestic Hotel. Modern detached, close to North Bay sands, team-making facilities all rooms, licensed, private bathrooms available, car park. Stamp please for brochure.

● The Sunday Mirror

Some years ago the children in my church organised an appeal to raise money to buy a guide dog for the blind. When all the money was in, arrangements were made to hand over the cheque to a representative of the association at a special service in church. As I made the presentation I heard myself saying:

'It gives me great pleasure, friends, to present this cheque to the association. The money the children have raised will buy a new blind dog for the guide…'

REVD J. DENNIS COPE, HARROGATE

nen catcher.

e at
of

me in
d of
ivate,
nent

y at
r of
No
larie
et.

I. B.
erre
48th
95.

Buffet is cancelled

This week's visit to the Royal Shakespeare Theatre, Stratford, by the Sadler's Wells Royal Ballet has been cancelled.

● Evesham Journal

PREGNANT

THE TOP TWENTY MALAPROPISMS

1 'We've recently bought a beautiful three piece suite in stimulated leather...'

2 'Of course, we'll be quite comfortable, he's on a granulated pension.'

3 'There's nothing I like more on an evening like this than a long cool John Thomas.'

4 'I told him a hundred times it was no use, but it was like duck's water off his back.'

5 'His mother told him always to masturbate thirty-two times before swallowing.'

6 'He's in considerable pain because of his swollen tentacles.'

250

7 'My niece
is going to apply for a divorce because her
marriage has never been consumed.'

8 'He had to get
his biceps right down my throat.'

9 'And they brought gifts – Gold,
Frankenstein and Myrrh.'

10 'I simply cannot stand
the new vicar – he fornicates all over you.'

11 'Does your headmaster
believe in capital punishment in the
classroom?'

12 'I think he's bitten off a bit
of a white elephant there.'

13 'I've got this blouse
with Border Anglesey around the neck.'

14 'She was walking down the aisle carrying the most beautiful bunch of friesans.'

15 'Ee, I'll be glad to get back on terra cotta again.'

16 'And so we switched on the emotion heater and went to bed.'

17 'He's wonderful for his age, you know. He has all his facilities.'

18 'I often walk through the students' compost.'

19 'Well, the ball's in your frying pan now.'

20 'Don't fly off at a tangerine, lad.'

'Private Lives'

IT is as delightful to have a play again at the **Duchess** (long occupied by nudists) as it is to see a charming revival of Noel Coward's "Private Lives."

As I have boasted before, I peeded over the side of my pram and actually saw Coward and Gertrude Lawrence create

● The Daily Telegraph

In Nottingham, travel agents

'**D**ear Miss,
Our Johnnie came home with a big hole in his trousers, will you please look into it.'

'**D**ear Miss,
I have not sent Johnny to school this morning because he hasn't been. I have given him something to make him go, and when he's been he'll come.'

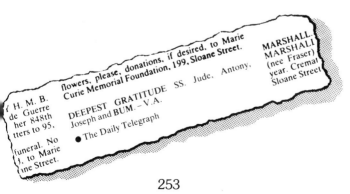

In 1965,
prior to a reception for Queen Elizabeth II outside
Bonn, West Germany's President Heinrich Lübke,
attempting an English translation of 'Gleich geht
es los' (It will soon begin), told the Queen:

'Equal goes it loose.'

Three years earlier, Lübke had greeted the
President of India at an airport by asking, instead
of 'How are you?':

'Who are you?'

(To which his guest replied: 'I am the President of
India.')

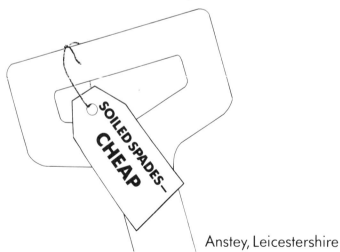

Anstey, Leicestershire

Priests

a time in prison could be a rewarding experience!

● The Church Times

Noel Coward, Beverley Nichols and Godfrey Winn were all invited to join Somerset Maugham at the Villa Mauresque to have lunch with the visiting American dramatist, Edna St Vincent Millay. As she swept on to the terrace overlooking the blue Mediterranean, she exclaimed:

'Oh Mr Maugham, but this is fairyland!'

WORD OF MOUTH

Apathy

SIR – Very nice to hear that someone is making an effort to tidy up Eckington.

Here in Kempsey there appears to be a state of apathy. The roadsides are a mass of weeds, the footpaths are overgrown, the delightful pond has flotsam and jetsam abounding. The council, in the modern sloppy manner, appear twice a year to have a good slash.

What has happened to the old pondsman? Knock off an odd bureaucrat and bring him back.

W. H. Whitehead

● The Evening News, Worcester

£200 Greek urn stolen

A GREEK urn worth £200 was stolen from St Osyth Priory on Tuesday by a visitor looking round the old building.

The vase, which belongs to the De Chair family, who live at the priory, is described as pottery, about 18 inches high, with two purple handles edged in gold.

The main body of the vase is purple with gold insets of nude women, and it is about eight inches wide at the wildest point.

● East Essex Gazette

Worried Ousden residents are praying for a bridge over troubled waters. If work on

256

**SURREY HEATH
BOROUGH COUNCIL**

HGV DRIVER/
OPERATOR

For the cesspool emptying and refuse collection service, presently based at Swift Lane Depot, Bagshot. Duties will include the emptying of cesspools and pail closets, care of the tanker vehicle and associated equipment, and also assisting in the refuse collection service when required. **A clean driving licence is essential.**

Arrangements had been made for us to meet up with another couple to go out together. My wife who was dressed up to the nines blurted out, 'We thought you'd get dressed up.' There was an awkward silence and then one of them replied dismally:

'We thought we had.'

PETER NELSON, HULL

Two friends of mine were with a group of people being shown round a stately home in Shropshire. On entering a particularly large room, the guide turned to his audience and said:

'This is where his lordship holds his balls and dances.'

IAN BURROW, TAUNTON

a bridge over troubled waters.

Joseph Conrad Walsh, 31, was found guilty of indecent exposure and carrying an offensive weapon when he first appeared at Redbridge Court on March 5.

● Ilford Recorder

BUSINESS at a crematorium chapel came to a

258

WORD OF MOUTH

"All you have to do is see a modest old lady undressing in a dormitory to realise that it is just not good enough and something must be done about it."

● Bridgnorth Journal

A MAN whose body was found in the sea at Penarth has been identified – almost

---

Tutor: Bob Wright MBOU

MIDLAND BIRDS

A refresher course for old or new course members. Detailed Tit study to be undertaken in Rugby as well as other field visits.

(EM) Fee £6.00

12 weekly meetings from 30th September

● Rugby Review

7.30–9.30 p.m.

---

flowers, please, donations, if desired, to ... Curie Memorial Foundation, 199, Sloane Street.

A DOCTOR, whose bedside manner was said to have the makings of a slapstick comedy, was found guilty of serious professional conduct by the General Medical Council Disciplinary Committee yesterday.

● The Daily Telegraph

The justice ministry has demanded a full ...

259

WORD OF MOUTH

STIMAȚI PASAGERI,

Pentru prevenirea unor eventuale pagube din incendii vă rugăm a respecta urmă-
toarele reguli:
1. Nu aruncați resturile de țigări la întâmplare și controlați acest lucru când părăsiți
camera.
2. Nu lăsați butelii cu gaze sau spraiuri lângă sursele de căldură.
3. Nu folosiți în camere aparate electrice personale, fără a înștiința electricianul de
serviciu sau pe administratorul de hotel.
4. În pădure, nu aruncați resturile de țigări sau chibrite aprinse în locuri nepermise.
Folosiți pentru fumat numai locurile marcate în acest scop.
5. Nu faceți foc în pădure sau în apropierea acesteia.
    În cazul unui incendiu sau început de incendiu, anunțați recepția hotelului sau pe
șeful unității cea mai apropiată.
    Telefonul pompierilor în Poiana-Brașov este 59 iar în Brașov 08.

DEAR GUTS,

    In order to prevent possible fire damages we kindly ask you to consider the fol-
lowing rules:
1. Do not throw cigarette ends at random and check this when leaving your room.
2. Do not keep sprays or butane fuel near heating sources.
3. Do not use personal electric equipment without announcing the electrician or the
reception.
4. Do not throw cigarette ends or matches in the forest. There are special signs
indicating the places where you can smoke.
5. Do not make fire in the forest or in the vicinity. In case of fire announce the
reception or the nearest office.
    In case of fire emergency phone, to 59 in Poiana-Brașov and 08 in Brașov.

DIRECȚIUNEA

● Rumanian Hotel

●●●●●● ●●● ●●●● ●●●●.

Mr Sid Weighell, general secretary of
the National Union of Railwaymen,
said yesterday: "You either have
regulations or you do not. If the
British Railways Board attempt to do
something with my member, I will
move right in to back him up."

● The Sunday Telegraph

The village of Lingdale was
quiet today.

including a karate expert and a rugby player—

Somerset's vital John Player League match with Kent at Taunton yesterday.

Seven arrests were made and police dogs were called in to patrol the boundaries. Fighting had broken out when police went to remove a group of youths from a toilet 20 yards from the boundary. The gates had been closed with a capacity 9,000 inside.

● The Daily Mail

In the days of the Commonwealth Office, the minister Arthur Bottomley paid a visit to Zambia in December 1965. In his public pronouncements he dismayed his hosts by referring to the country as:

'*Gambia.*'

'**M**r Ronald Reagan has lost his head over President Carter...er...Mr Ronald Reagan has lost his _lead_ over President Carter.'

BBC WORLD SERVICE NEWS, 20 AUGUST 1980

> **Assorted Tin Knickers**
> Originally £1.50.............................
> ● Torquay Evening Paper ....**Half Price 75p**

My wife, a school librarian,
was amused by the request of a rather small boy,
obviously sent by his teacher, who came into the
library and asked for a copy of:

'She Stoops to Conga.'

DAVID ALLSOPP, LONG EATON

'**I**n response to complaints
*from the touring company of <u>Oh Calcutta</u>, the
nude revue, that they were suffering from the
cold, the theatre management has agreed to
install fan heaters.'*

BBC RADIO 4 NEWS, 12 DECEMBER 1981

WORD OF MOUTH

Hubert Humphrey
commented on a failed attempt to assassinate
President Gerald R. Ford, thus:

*'There are too many guns in the hands of people
who don't know how to use them.'*

President Ford himself once commented:

*'Mr Nixon was the thirty-seventh President of
the United States. He had been preceded by
thirty-six others.'*

SWIMMING
POOL
PEDESTRIANS ONLY

Golspie, Scotland

263

WORD OF MOUTH

$\mathbf{A}$t my father's funeral,
my step-mother had allowed one of father's
friends to say "a few words" after the service was
over. He started by saying that the last time he had
been at that crematorium there had been some
swallows flying about. He then went on to say how
he had gone on bird-watching expeditions with my
father, and so on. He ended (the cremation was
taking place in early January) by saying:

*'Now Mr G — and the swallows have
departed to a warmer climate.'*

REVD P. G., OXFORD

Both extracts are sold in spray
atomisers and are certain to
evoke the tradition of the
English countryside, providing a
stable fragrance which lasts
throughout the day.

At the Royal Wedding in July, 1981, Lady Diana Spencer vowed: 'I, Diana Frances, take thee Philip Charles Arthur George to my wedded husband' – accidentally transposing the first two of his Royal collection of names. Not to be outdone, Prince Charles, instead of saying 'and all my worldly goods with thee I share' vowed 'with all *thy* goods with thee I share.'

While holidaying
in a small village in Scotland I was speaking to an
elderly inhabitant who had had a day out in
Edinburgh. At one point she said:

*'I wanted to cross the road, but I dinna ken how
to work the Presbyterian Crossing.'*

HELEN KERR GREEN, MARKET DRAYTON

'We are
examing alternative anomalies.'

WILLIAM WHITELAW, HOUSE OF COMMONS,
1 DECEMBER 1981

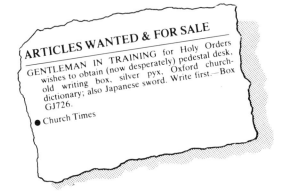

ARTICLES WANTED & FOR SALE

GENTLEMAN IN TRAINING for Holy Orders
wishes to obtain (now desperately) pedestal desk,
old writing box, silver pyx, Oxford church-
dictionary; also Japanese sword. Write first.—Box
GJ726.

● Church Times

In the December 1981 edition of *The Atlantic Monthly,* David Stockman, Director of the Office of Management and Budget in the Reagan Administration was quoted on the following topics:

On Reaganomics:
'The reason we did it wrong – not wrong, but less than the optimum – was that we said, Hey, we have to get a programme out fast... we didn't think it all the way through. We didn't add up all the numbers.'

On the Administration's budget:
'None of us really understands what's going on with these numbers.'

On defence spending:
'The whole question is blatant inefficiency, poor deployment of manpower, contracting idiocy.'

On his recommendations
for cuts in Social Security benefits:
'Basically I screwed up quite a bit.'

He offered his resignation.

'**W**e are going to play
a hiding and finding game. Now, are your balls
high up or low down? Close your eyes a minute
and dance around, and look for them. Are they
high up? Or are they low down? If you have
found your balls, toss them over your shoulder
and play with them.'

FROM A BBC 'MUSIC AND MOVEMENT' PROGRAMME FOR
CHILDREN WHICH, HAPPILY FOR POSTERITY, IS STILL ON
RECORD

Francesca Bellere is refusing to disclose the father's identity.

NEW YORK CURB ON GREEDY UNDERTAKERS
By Our New York Staff

Efforts are being made in New York
to stop undertakers charging the
earth for burials.

● The Daily Telegraph

Defender

In 1966, George Brown
who had formerly run the Department of
Economic Affairs was winding up for the Labour
Government in a debate on the economy in the
House of Commons. He declared earnestly:

*'For almost two years now we have tried to
manage the economy in a way that no economy
has ever been managed before.'*

Two mothers chatting
about a recently held Fancy Dress Party. One
asked: 'And did your little daughter enjoy
herself?'
The other replied:

*'Oh, yes, she looked very sweet. We dressed her
up in one of those Japanese commodes.'*

PAM FOX, WORPLESDON

JEAN SIBELIUS

UNFAITHFUL

By Dr. FRANK S. CAPRIO

Why married couples cheat, with many case histories, by a writer with a wide reputation in this field.

● Publishers List

Tone Poem, "Lemminkäinen's Return," Opus 22 N~ · '~om "Four Legends"\

One afternoon during the long, hot summer of '76, a group of us were digesting a large lunch. A large well-endowed lady with a penchant for wearing loose thick wooly jumpers complained that the heat was overbearing. I said:

'That's hardly surprising. What do you expect with your big sweaty floppers…?'

JOHN CARTER, CARDIFF

I met a woman whose husband was in hospital and asked how he was. She replied:

'Not good. They gave him a post mortem yesterday.'

JOAN HEWITT, MARYPORT

WORD OF MOUTH

stolen

o by
ray,
Bal-
Sea

pold

n
AN

A W
held i
nearly
on M
Em
were
tigatio
France
close t
The
a full
makes
Italy's
impre

POST DATE

NEWTON Abbot's new post office will open on September 3, provided there are no snags.

One innovation will be a single-queueing system, where customers line up behind a barrier and only move forward to the counter when a widow becomes free.

● Mid-Devon Advertiser

● The

BOOSE
Hampsh
Ethel T
donatio
Fund or

BINGE
home,
Marga

the
per

the

a

Female

Worried Ousden residents are praying for a bridge over troubled waters. If work on replacing the narrow hump-backed bride over the River Kennett is not completed soon, they fear there will be traffic chaos.

● Bury Free Press

Traffic will hit

Her Majesty the Queen,
reading a speech during her Australian tour in
1977, referred to:

'The twenty-fifth reign of my year.'

(Shortly afterwards she started wearing
spectacles to read.)

272

Nice! Brucie is a grandad

ENTERTAINER Bruce Forsyth has become a grandfather.

His 22-year-old daughter, Julie, has given birth to a baby boy. She has named him Luke.

Bruce's latest addition to the generation game weighed in at 6lb 13 oz.

Luke's father, 29-year-old Dominic Grant, said: "It's terrific. I don't even know what lay it is."

● The Daily Mail

I cringe even as I write this down…
I was talking to a widow and asked her when her
husband died. She replied: 'Eleven years ago – on
12 August.' Without a moment's hesitation, – and
as the words sprang from my lips, I could taste
shoe-leather – I said:

'Oh – the Glorious Twelfth!'

PAUL JACOBSON, LEEDS

WORD OF MOUTH

When I was in pantomine
at Peterborough, I had to run on the stage at a very
dramatic moment and announce to the King: 'Your
daughter has been taken away by gruesome
demons!' Instead, I rushed on stage and said:

*'Your daughter has been taken away by
greesome nuemons!'*

AUDREY LENO, EWELL

FAMILY
PLANNING.

PLEASE USE REAR
ENTRANCE

Barnstable Health Centre

TOMMY HARRIS
FUNERAL DIRECTOR
9 BROAD ST., STAPLE HILL
Tel. 569479
Special rates for
old-age pensioners.

In the 1930s
radio announcer Harry von Zell (who later
appeared in the Burns and Allen television shows)
was due to introduce a broadcast by President
Hoover. The words that actually came out of his
mouth were:

*'Ladies and gentlemen. The President of the
United States — Hoobert Heever!'*

WORD OF MOUTH

A canticle is a sacred song used in church services and a New Testament canticle would be such a song deriving from the New Testament, e.g. 'My soul doth magnify the Lord'. One day at theological college some years ago, a lecturer marched in and announced he would address us on the subject of:

'New Cantament Testicles.'

REVD A. C. BETTS, LEEDS

this field.

Mixed sessions planned for Leicester sauna

The mixed saunas will be held two days a week.

City council leader the Rev. Ken Middleton, who is vicar of St. Matthews Church in Taylor Road, said: "I should think this is all right as long as people are fully clothed.

● Leicester Mercury

Are your cook's

John Gielgud went to see the first performance of Richard Burton's *Hamlet*. According to the story, the performance was not of the highest but nevertheless Gielgud felt obliged to go back stage and congratulate Burton whilst concealing his true feelings about what he had seen. On entering Burton's dressing room, he discovered that the actor was in a state of undress. Gielgud meant to say, 'I'll come back when you're dressed.' What he is reported to have said, was:

'I'll come back when you're better…'

4.15 THE SKY AT NIGHT: Voyager 2 reaches Jupiter, with Patrick Moore.
● The Daily Mail

WORD OF MOUTH

Leeds call girl raped. Man aids police

● Leeds Evening Post

Take the family to
**Birtsmorton Water
Foul Sanctuary near
Malvern**

● The Hereford Ad mag

$\mathbf{A}$t a promotional evening
for the Berlin Tourist Board, I was asked by a
German official, 'Have you ever been to Berlin?'
Without thinking, I heard myself answer:

*'No, but my father often flew over it
during the war.'*

LEN EDEN, BIRMINGHAM

CARTER ORDERED TO REST
By Our Washington Staff

President Carter was ordered to rest
by a doctor for what was described as
an aggravated problem with haemor-
rhoids.

A White House spokesman said
that Mr Carter had been in discom-
fort for several days and had been
told by his personal physician, Rear
Admiral William Lukash, to rest so
that he could seek relief from pain.

● The Daily Telegraph

...usden residents are praying

MANURE
75p per bag
DO IT YOURSELF
50p per bag

Sussex

An old lady
was telling her friend about a
'Good Companions' party:

*'And then they gave us some
Round-About-Eight-O'clock mints.*

WENDY HAMMOND, BOURNEMOUTH

The
open mouth invites the foot.

ANON

Dentopedalogy is the science
of opening your mouth and putting your foot in it.
I've been practising it for years.

PRINCE PHILIP

That is not what I meant at all.
That is not it, at all.

T. S. ELIOT, *THE LOVE SONG OF J. ALFRED PRUFROCK*

A *blooper*
is worse than a *goof*, more adult than a *boo-boo*,
not as serious as a *blunder*, equivalent to a *gaffe*.
Repeated commission of any results in a
description of having *Foot in Mouth Disease*.

WILLIAM SAFIRE, *SAFIRE'S POLITICAL DICTIONARY*

Babes
and
Sucklings

In memory of my mother who heard the peculiar things I said as a child and, thankfully, kept them to herself.

And when the chief priests and scribes saw the wonderful things that he did, and the children crying in the temple, and saying, Hosanna to the Son of David; they were sore displeased, and said unto him, Hearest thou what these say? And Jesus saith unto them, Yea; have ye never read, Out of the mouth of babes and sucklings thou hast perfected praise?

St Matthew 21 : 15 (quoting Psalm 8 : 2)

All the universal experience of the ages, showing that imperceptibly children do grow from the cradle to manhood, did not exist for the countess. Her son's progress towards manhood at each of its stages had seemed as extraordinary as though there had never been millions and millions of human beings who had gone through the same process.

Tolstoy

They tell me too of their last-born: the clever thing the darling child said yesterday, and how much more wonderful or witty or quaint it is than any child that ever was born before. And I have to pretend to be surprised, delighted, interested; though

285

the last child is like the first, and has said and done nothing that did not delight Adam and me when you and Abel said it. For you were the first children in the world, and filled us with such wonder and delight as no couple can ever again feel while the world lasts.

Shaw, Back to Methuselah
(Eve to Cain)

What is a 'Babe and Suck'? This collection
defines it as a remark – smart, innocent,
precocious or sweet – made by a child. The
most likely age at which a quotable saying
will fall from the lips of a child appears to
be around four but I have also included
several from young people to whom the
word 'babe' could hardly be applied, and
certainly not the word 'suckling'.

What is the attraction of such sayings?
Their charm stems mainly from the faintly
ludicrous way in which childlike minds are
brought to bear upon adult concerns.
Grown-ups have enough difficulty with
complicated matters like religion and sex.
No wonder the innocent eye or ear of a
child can make so much more sense of
them – sense, of a kind.

As a child I was convinced that when a
lesson was read in church the reader
always called it 'God's Holy Golf-ball'. All
children make the sound of words fit the
sense in their heads. The logic of my hearing was confirmed for me by the fact that
the lectern eagle was quite clearly standing on the Holy Golf-ball.

Allowing the imagination to invent its

287

own meanings for sounds before we have been directed by the written word is not, of course, solely an aptitude that children have. I heard of a grandmother who was convinced that the 'girl with kaleidoscope eyes' in the Beatles' song 'Lucy in the Sky with Diamonds' was really the 'girl with colitis goes by'. But it is an important point of departure for many of the sayings in this book. There can be few who have not heard of the little boy who called his teddy bear 'Gladly' because of the line in the hymn which goes (for childish ears, at least) 'Gladly, my cross-eyed bear . . .'

After perception of words, the perception of behaviour and situations is the next most promising area for a junior *bon mot*. Many years ago when Nancy Astor was standing for Parliament in a Plymouth constituency, she was advised that it would make a good impression in the poorer districts if she were to be escorted by someone in naval uniform. Accordingly, on one occasion, she went canvassing down one of the seedier streets with a well-built bluejacket at her side. When Lady Astor knocked on one door and asked of the scruffy little boy who answered it whether Mummy was at home, she got the reply: 'No, but she said you could have the back bedroom and leave half a crown on the table.'

It is not just simple misapprehension

that makes many of the examples in this collection amusing to the adult, however. At times, a kind of illumination is spread which few adults would be capable of. The young Princesses, Elizabeth and Margaret, apparently coined for George V the appropriate epithet 'Grandpa England'. Charles Lamb, as a boy in the 1780s, remarked to his sister, on observing the fulsome epitaphs in a churchyard: 'Mary, where are all the naughty people buried?'

At other times, we delight in the sayings of children because they express what we would wish to say but which we are prevented from doing because of peculiar adult notions of taste. The young Viscount Eversley, on hearing Charles James Fox speak in Parliament, exclaimed: 'What is that fat gentleman in such a passion about?' John Mortimer, the playwright and QC, once overheard his 7-year-old daughter discussing with a friend what they were going to be when they grew up. Said she: 'One thing I'm *not* going to be . . . and that's a member of the public.'

Actress Judi Dench's daughter Finty looked like following in her mother's footsteps one Christmas when she landed the part of 'The Innkeeper's Wife' in a school nativity play. For weeks, her parents heard nothing but the lines of the Innkeeper's Wife repeated day in, day out. A visitor to the house asked what sort of play was it she was in. What was it about? Finty replied: 'Well, it's about this Innkeeper's Wife...'

The question must be asked, though, whether remarks treasured by doting parents should be passed on. Do they appear quite so amusing and wonderful to other people? As, at the time of writing, I don't have any children of my own to speak of I think I may be allowed to say 'Yes'. Nevertheless, I can still cringe when too much significance is attached to them. In an essay on Miles Davis, the jazz trumpeter, Kenneth Tynan quoted his 9-year-old daughter who explained how she knew a Davis recording when she heard one: 'Because,' she said, 'it sounds like a little boy who's been locked out and wants to get in.'

As Anthony Hope exclaimed at the first night of *Peter Pan* – 'Oh, for an hour of Herod!' *Peter Pan* was concocted in part from the countless children's remarks assiduously jotted down in notebooks by J. M. Barrie.

I hope the choice of remarks in this little collection will have a less grating effect. The sayings have largely been contributed by listeners to the BBC radio programme *Quote ... Unquote*. Where attributions are given, I am grateful for being given permission to print. I hope that what was said, in many cases, a number of years ago will not embarrass the speaker now that he or she has put away childish things. If it does, then don't blame me, blame your doting parents or grandparents. Where ages are given, these are at the time when the remark was first uttered.

Where no attribution is given, the 'Babe and Suck' may have reached me from any number of sources. There is a sprinkling taken from a booklet called *Never Forget the Children* published by the Pre-School Playgroups Association and some more from a one shilling paperback published in 1895 with the title *Quaint Sayings and Odd Notions of Children (with Reminiscences of my own Childhood)* by David Macrae. Others are from the common stock of 'traditional' sayings which – as I found when compiling my earlier book, *Eavesdroppings* – does not prevent people from claiming them as their own. The age-old remark from a little girl to a little boy when he dropped his trousers – 'My, that's a handy little gadget!' – has reached me from several sources. One says it involved 'the daughter of a friend', another says 'it was told me by a friend who was a teacher about the local primary school at which he taught', and a third specifically says it concerned 'our 2-year-old son'.

My explanation for this phenomenon is that 'personalising' stories is an accepted way of making them – and jokes – more compelling. Why else does the comedian frequently say, 'My wife, she's so fat ...' when he may not have a wife at all, let alone a fat one? Still, I believe that most of the remarks recorded here did genuinely come out of the mouths of babes and sucklings at one time or another.

Some give us an intriguing glimpse into other people's family lore. Many of the remarks have been treasured and endlessly repeated over the years within the family circle and now will find a larger audience. For many years in my own family we used the expression 'Don't go through a field with a bull in it!' when one member was inclined to rub another up the wrong way. This stemmed from an incident on holiday in North Wales when, as a small boy, I had indeed encouraged the family to go through a field with a large bull in it. Unfortunately, such remarks can require a great deal of explanation and mean very little to those outside the family.

Taken as a whole, what does *Babes and Sucklings* show us? A number of things. That parents should be constantly aware that Big Ears Is Listening To You. That God would never have invented breastfeeding if he had not intended confusion to be spread in childish minds. And, above all, that the best remarks recorded here were quite clearly spoken by persons young enough to know better.

292

I took my children to the circus for the first time a few years ago. One of the acts was a troupe of performing elephants. They walked along a bench about one foot high and one foot wide. My 4-year-old daughter gazed at this for a while and then remarked scornfully:

'**I could do** *that***!**'

> *Andrew Griffiths, Surbiton*

'. . . mind the tree! . . . look out, don't hit the settee! . . . mind my doll! . . .'

WORD OF MOUTH

While working in the garden, unseen by the tots next door, I overheard the following game of 'Mothers and Fathers' in progress. One little 4-year-old girl was dressed in nurse's cap and apron. Another was struggling to fix a pillow under the front of her dress. A 5-year-old boy had just fastened on his dog collar and taken a prayer book out of the props basket. He turned round with a disgusted look on his face when he saw what the girls were doing. He said:

'You've got it all wrong. It's weddings first, babies afterwards.'
Ethel A. Crowther, Dunstable

A small child overheard in church:

'Our father, chart in heaven, hullo how be you then?'
Eleanor Clarke, North Tawton

Small boy watching my uncle, then a corporal, putting on his uniform before returning to his unit:

'Gosh! I bet you're the smartest soldier in your fort!'
Miss P. Simson, Mere

WORD OF MOUTH

I was walking with my parents along the seafront in Norfolk. We had with us our two dogs, a labrador and a dachshund. A little girl, walking in the other direction, commented:

'Look at that dog, Mummy, he's worn his legs right down to the ground.'

Sheila Gilbert-Hill, Flitwick

A small boy was standing in a bus queue behind a smartly dressed woman with a fox fur slung over her shoulder. The head of the unfortunate animal was hanging down her back. This fascinated the small boy who, having walked round the front, looked up at the woman and said:

'Did your dog die?'

Mary Lawless, Glossop

Years ago, I overheard my children playing 'I Spy'. One said, 'I spy with my little eye something beginning with "U".' The reply came – 'Onions.' Said the first child:

'Yes, now it's your turn . . .'

Mrs J. M. Knight, Bexhill-on-Sea

WORD OF MOUTH

Heard on a local bus – a young mother was breast-feeding her baby during the journey and was seen by a small boy who said, 'Mum, what's that baby doing?' 'Having its dinner,' replied Mum. Said the small boy:

'Oooh! Has he got to eat all that before he gets to Barnsley?'
Mrs A. White, Barnsley

Oliver, almost 5 years old, had a finger firmly wedged inside his left nostril. His mother admonished him. Oliver explained:

'I wasn't picking it. I was resting my finger up it.'

Two little girls were running down the road, obviously having missed the school bus. One of them slowed down and said to her sister, 'Let's stop and say a prayer that we won't be late for school.' The other, more practical, replied:

'I've got a better idea. We'll keep on running and pray as we go along.'
Margaret Beaumont, Kenilworth

296

How's this for a muddle? My mother asked a little 5-year-old, 'And how is your kitten?' The girl replied:

'Quite well, thank you. When it is 4-months-old it has got to go to the dentist to be made into a he.'
Miss M. Sanders, Hove

My friend's little girl, aged 4:

'Mummy, I love you so much that when you die I am going to have you stuffed!'
Freda Skinner, Putney

Our 4-year-old son after many hours trying to ride a bike was heard praying fiercely skywards:

'God – if – you – don't – teach – me – to – ride – this – bike – I'll – get – a – long – long – ladder –and – I'll – get – a – big – axe –and – I'll – climb – up – and – chop –your – head – off!'

(The awful part is, he learnt to ride it the very next day.)
Tricia Catchpole, Woodbridge

Half-time at a football match on a hot afternoon – one short-sighted youth removed his very thick-lensed glasses to give them a wipe. His friend on taking them from him and trying them out was heard to comment:

'Good God, you must have good eye-sight to see through these!'
Isobel E. Breheny, Tewkesbury

My sister was listening to her two grand-children playing at a make-believe tea-party. Ann, aged 6, and Sarah, 4, had a baby sister who was still being breast-fed. When the choice of what they would have to eat arose (both having a fascinating lisp), Ann said:

'We'll give them Marmite thand-wiches and some chocolate bithkits. But what can we give the baby 'cos she only eats boothums and we haven't got any?'
Winifred Lewis, Poole

Child 1: 'I know how to find out our teacher's age.'
Child 2: 'How?'
Child 1: 'Look in her knickers. In mine it says "4 to 5 years".'

Overheard as two 9-year-old boys walked out of school one afternoon discussing a lesson – one said, 'It was *so boring*!' The other agreed:

'Crumbs, yes, it was nearly as boring as watching Annabelle undressing.'
Valerie Philpott, Faversham

A friend was helping some 9-year-old boys revise for a forthcoming maths exam. Several of them seemed quite lost on the topic of ratios and so the teacher asked the class as a whole, 'Does anybody know what a ratio is?' Convinced he was on the right lines, a voice piped up:

'Please, miss, I think he was a sailor.'
Derek Lamb, Potters Bar

As a nanny, I was listening to two little girls in the bath. 'Well, I keeping asking,' said one, 'what is this hole in my tummy?' Reply from the other:

'If you really want to know, that's where God poked you to see if you were done.'
Mrs F. Dee, Kingston-upon-Thames

'It's a single-parent f

'...a social worker.'

A 7-year-old boy was watching the TV news coverage of the Queen's departure for her tour of Arabia in 1979. Said he:

'Look Mum, the Queen's going ... now we can do what we want.'
Michael Frater, West Bridgford

After a lesson on the Magnificat, children in a Sunday School class had been asked to do some work on this theme. One child drew a picture of an old man surrounded by hundreds of black dots. When the teacher asked what this was, the child replied:

'Abraham and his seed forever.'
Canon Eric Allen, Settle

A quote from my 5½-year-old grand-daughter to her mother:

'I shall never be able to be dead as I could not keep still long enough.'
Ruth Roberts, Brandon

Father to small son: 'Do you know what you want for tea?' Small son to father:

'Yes ... lots!'
J. R. Norden, Brackley

I had scolded my eldest child (aged 5) and her sister for getting into mischief and I told them to find something to do. Just as I was leaving the room I heard the eldest say to her sister:

'Come on, Pippa. Let's go upstairs and watch Nanny putting her teeth in.'

Mrs G. A. Harris, Ware

Two schoolboys on the top of a bus. First boy: 'If there was another war, you would be much better off than me.' Surprised and intrigued, the second boy asked why. Said the first:

'Because you have got me for a friend, but I have only got you.'

Mrs M. Law, East Twickenham

A schoolboy came home complaining that he had to do drama:

'It's a horrid play, but I've got the best bit. I have to say, "Bubble, bubble, toilet trouble." '

WORD OF MOUTH

Two grey-suited small boys were waiting outside the restaurant in Harrods and one said seriously to the other:

'The trouble is that she *will* **keep buying Utrillos.'**
Elspeth Walder, Blackburn

On a sailing holiday in August 1939, we came across a fishing boat on the stocks with a happy sailor singing loudly, leaning against the bows. Another man was passing by and his very small son asked:

'Are there two sorts of drink, Daddy – one to make you sing and one to make you swear?'
Brian Baskin, Leigh-on-Sea

Some years ago I was riding on a bus in Peterborough. Many of the passengers were schoolgirls who were busily tearing open their end of term reports and one girl shouted the following to a friend at the far end of the bus:

'Cor, Carol, I'm come top in English and Speech. And I ain't never come top in nothing before.'
Mrs J. Hoffman, Holton cum Beckering

My daughter speaking to a friend about a girl who was presumably in their form at school:

'She's so awful – even her friends don't like her.'
Mrs M. Hall, Macclesfield

At a Catholic convent school in Sydney, I once heard a brand new pupil aged about 5 express the most un-catholic sentiment at morning prayers in the chapel. She began:

'Our Father, who aren't in heaven, hullo, what is your name?'
Sue Merricks, Torpoint

During a Religious Knowledge lesson based on the Ten Commandments, the teacher attempted to skirt round any discussion of 'Thou shalt not commit adultery.' Imagine her relief when David, a 7-year-old farmer's son, insisted on giving his interpretation:

'It means, miss, you shouldn't put water with the milk.'
D. D. Jones, Northwich

WORD OF MOUTH

On Hallowe'en night, my daughter (aged 7) heard somebody quote the rhyme about 'ghoulies and ghosties and long-leggety beasties/And things that go bump in the night' and went away to draw a picture. Some time later she came rushing in and announced:

'I've drawn a picture of some ghosties and they've all got ghoulies!'

Liz Crosby, West Malling

My 2-year-old grandson's main joy in life is eating! Then he saw snow for the first time. After it had been falling all night, I carried him to the window, pulled back the curtain – and there, in all its glory, was a huge hill covered in thick, glistening snow. Eyes shining, Dylan said:

'Ooh! Cake!'

Iris Bryce, Borough Green

Having just been introduced to a friend's young son, I inquired, 'How old are you, Peter?' 'Five,' he replied. 'When will you be six?' I asked. Came the reply:

'When I'm bigger.'

A. Coles, Coventry

I overheard a small boy on the train talking to his mother about a recent stay he had made at a friend's house. 'They've got a lovely new bath,' he said. When his mother asked how he knew it was a *new* bath, the boy replied:

'Well, it didn't have *any* **tide marks round it.'**

Miss M. O'Beirne, Moreton

A mother who had knitted her 5-year-old boy a 'V'-neck sweater was puzzled by his refusal to consider wearing it. Finally, the reason became clear:

'I don't want one like that. My teacher has one and when she bends down – you can see her lungs.'

Shortly before the birth of my second son, my elder son (aged $3\frac{1}{2}$) wandered into my bedroom. Catching sight of my bare bosom, he asked, 'What are those things?' To the best of my ability, I explained that when the new baby arrived, I should be able to provide milk for him or her. He gave me a long serious look and added:

'How're you going to get those corks out?'

Dorothy Alt, Bury St Edmunds

I was driving my 11-year-old daughter to her very first term at boarding school in the south of England, wretchedly aware that I had made a complete hash of telling her the facts of life the night before. In increasing embarrassment, I embarked yet again on the topic, the tense little white face beside me betraying no response until at last I burst out with, 'Darling, we haven't much longer – if there's anything you don't understand – anything at all – *do* ask me now. I'll answer everything you care to ask!' She said:

'There *is* **one thing, Mummy. I simply can't** *begin* **to fathom the Holy Trinity.'**

Monica Fletcher, Tadcaster

In Victorian times, the children of Lord Lytton were putting on a game of charades for a house party. The scene for one of the words was a Crusader's return from the wars and showed his wife meeting him at the castle gates. He told her of his triumphs and then the little girl who was playing his wife pointed to a very large row of dolls, in all shapes and sizes, laid out in a row. She said:

'And I, too, my Lord, have not been idle while you've been away.'

I was clearing up the bathroom from the deluge resulting from the bath of Simon (4) and Sarah (2). They had gone into my bedroom and were evidently in front of the long mirror, for I heard Simon say:

'Now *you* spit, Sarah, and *I* can be the windscreen wiper.'
Annette Mann, Wombourne

When my daughter started school, one of her teachers was six feet tall and another was only five foot. One day I overheard my girl singing the following hymn in bed:

**'All things bright and beautiful,
All *teachers* great and small . . .'**
Mrs A. M. Mitchell, Saundersfoot

A small boy was taken out to tea by his parents at a neighbour's house. Also present at the meal was the neighbour's lodger. As soon as the meal began the boy began to stare at the lodger. In spite of several words of correction, the boy continued to stare. Finally, the boy's father asked, 'Why on earth are you staring at Mr Jones?' The boy answered:

'Well, I can't see that he drinks like a fish.'

On the day that I returned from hospital with the newest member of the family, my 5-year-old daughter, Sally, watched in amazement as I began to breast-feed. She burst out laughing, falling to the floor in helpless mirth, just managing to point and splutter, 'She's ... she's ... biting your bust!' I tried to explain, but more was to come when I proceeded to put the baby to the other breast. 'No, no,' said Sally, 'don't let her bite that one.' I explained that the baby had to feed from both but Sally was not convinced:

'No, no, you'd better save that one for tomorrow.'

Caryl Yendell, Leeds

My 10-year-old son was watching *World of Sport* on ITV a year or two ago and asked me:

'Is Dickie Davies a descendant of The Mallens?'

Sheila Davies, Wrexham

A child at prayer:

'Give us this day our daily bread – *and butter!'*

310

Me to my 6-year-old niece, 'If you were my little girl, I'd send you to boarding school.' My niece:

'If you were my Mummy, my Mummy would be my Auntie and I'd run away and go and live with her.'
Miss P. R. Shorey, Westerham

My 5-year-old came home and told me that he and a friend had found a book down in the meadows full of people with no clothes on. 'Really!' said I.

'Yes, nothing on at all – and the sun wasn't even shining.'
Mrs J. D. Fortune, Stretford

Our son, aged 20 months, went out for a walk in the woods nearby with his mother and sister. Suddenly he saw a dalmatian coming down the path towards him. Instantly, he became very concerned, pointed at the new arrival, and said:

'Dog . . . bit burnt!'
Norman and Jenny Skillen,
Bochum, West Germany

WORD OF MOUTH

My brother's name is Attila. He's 7 years old. I eavesdropped on a conversation he had with another boy, Kenneth, of the same age. Attila asked, 'Do you reckon you will get married when you grow up?' Said Kenneth:

'No! I'd rather become a policeman.'
J. Pusztai, Seven Hills, NSW

A very tall man looked down at my very small son and asked, 'What's your name?' 'Alex,' said my small son. 'Alex what?' Came the serious reply:

'--ander.'
A. R. Mills, Woodford Green

Back during my schooldays, the teacher had left the room and we were all working quietly except the class bully who turned to his friend and said:

'I dunno what I've done to my 'and, but everytime I 'it someone it really 'urts.'
Elliott Manley, Haslemere

Our neighbour's children watched this year's Boat Race avidly and while the 4-year-old shouted for Oxford, the 6-year-old was screaming support for:

'Sainsbury's!'

My mother teaches a second year class at a primary school. If a child arrives during the year she tries to discover his or her capabilities as tactfully as possible. When David arrived, she thought she would test his arithmetic by becoming a customer while he was serving at the toy shop. She read out a list of what she wanted and he fetched them eagerly – a great honour to serve teacher! – but when it came to adding up the bill he looked blank and then panic-stricken. The rest of the class fell silent. It was a tense moment. Then with sudden relief he gasped:

'You can have them for nothing, Mrs Coutts!'

Catriona Ogilvie, Lutterworth

A 9-year-old's answer to a scripture question:

'There were ten bridesmaids and five were virgins and five were careful.'

Recovering in hospital from a gall bladder operation, I received a visit from a small person on her way to see another patient. She peeped into my room and after carefully considering my blue slippers for a while she confided in me that her Mummy had similar ones. 'Are you visiting your Daddy?' I asked. Came the reply:

'Yes – he's got hailstones – and a big scarf on his side.'
Patricia Gale, Flackwell Heath

This was overheard by a teacher on a school trip to the zoo. Two 6-year-old lads were looking up at a giraffe. One said:

'Cor, 'asn't 'e got a long way to wee!'
Rowena Thomas, Wrexham

Returning home through the back streets one afternoon, I noticed two youngsters, aged about 9 or 10, coming towards me, arms round each other's shoulders, heads close together, and deep in conversation. As they passed me, I heard one boy say to the other:

'Wot you rarver 'ave? Slit froat or stab in the back?'
L. E. Desmond, St John's Wood

314

A friend's child would persist in swearing and, to try and make him stop it, he was told that Jesus was always with him and knew everything he said and didn't like little boys swearing. It seemed to work for a time until one day he was riding his tricycle and his mother heard him say:

'Hold tight, Jesus, we're going round this bloody corner.'
Mrs M. R. Healey, Daresbury

*'Quite a good Christmas, really –
my new Mum is much better than the
one Dad had last year.'*

I met my friend's little girl, aged 4, just after the birth of her baby brother. I myself was very large and pregnant. She eyed me, thoughtfully, and then asked kindly:

'Why don't you have yours out?'
Eileen Hocking, Falmouth

A small boy had been particularly naughty so his father gave him a good smack bottom and sent him up to his room. After a while, as everything seemed to be quiet, he thought he had better go and investigate. On opening the door he saw his small son with his back to the mirror, holding up his shirt tail surveying himself. With tears in his eyes, he turned to his father and said:

'You've cracked it!'
Mrs C. Joynson, Horley

I was having tea with a family and the little boy asked his Mummy if he could have another biscuit. She replied, 'Not another, dear, you've already had several.' Said he:

'Well, could I just *borrow* it for a few minutes?'
Ella Reynolds, Chesham

316

A family joke: some years ago when my daughter, Anne, was 7 years old, she came out of school saying the girls had been colouring their paintings. 'What about the boys?' I asked innocently. She said:

'Oh, they're varnishing their wilburs.'

(We have since realised that Wilbur was a friendly pig.)
Margaret Coatworth, Middlesbrough

My son rushed in from the garden shouting:

'Mummy, mummy, there's a nose-pecker on our apple tree.'
Ailsa Boyle, Twyford

When my son (then aged $2\frac{1}{2}$) saw me breast-feeding his brand new baby sister, he looked horrified and asked what I was doing. When I told him that I was giving the baby her dinner, he looked even more horrified and said:

'Oh, don't let her eat that!'
Mrs E. F. Cole, Bournemouth

317

The parents of a 4-year-old child had installed a two-way baby alarm system with a speaker in the child's room and another downstairs. You could communicate in either direction. One night a baby-sitter was having dinner when the child woke up in the middle of the meal. The girl called up, 'Johnny, are you all right?' Silence. She called again, 'Johnny, are you all right?' Silence. So she thought she had better go upstairs. Still complete silence. She was just about to open the door of the bedroom when she heard Johnny say:

'What do you want, wall?'

I overheard my two small daughters talking. One said:

'Don't let's ask Mummy – she'll only say "No" – let's ask Daddy.'
Jane Cliff, Hove

My 3-year-old daughter was asked if she had a Grandpa. She thought for a bit and then replied:

'Oh, yes, we've got one of those at my Granny's house.'
Mrs V. Carter, Colchester

Uncle John was lathering his cheek prior to shaving:

'O Mamma, Uncle John is brushing his teeth all over his face.'

Overheard: a small boy who had apparently fallen out with one of his equally small girlfriends. His mother pointed out that it was Catherine's birthday next week and asked what he was going to give her. 'Action Man,' he said. His mum pointed out: 'But she won't like that.' Said he:

'I *know.'*

Daphne Clarke, Durham

A little boy was looking through the sitting room window and watching a funeral cortège outside a neighbour's house opposite. That night his mother said to him, 'Your prayers are very short tonight.' He explained why:

'Yes, you see, because God was very busy unpacking Mrs Jones from across the road.'

Joy Longhurst, Canterbury

319

WORD OF MOUTH

My 10-year-old granddaughter was trying to describe a buxom friend of her mother's to another girl. 'You know her, she's W.A.D.,' she explained. 'What's W.A.D.?' asked the other.

'It's what Daddy says – she's Well and Dowd.'

Joan Hunt, Birmingham

A newly married couple, having just left the church, were being photographed while surrounded by the guests. A small girl was heard to ask her mother:

'Does he give her some of his pollen now or will he wait until later?'

A young mother (a cousin of mine, actually) had the misfortune to upset the milk jug while having tea with her 4-year-old daughter. 'Damn!' she exlaimed. 'Oh, poor Mummy!' said the girl. 'Shall I fetch a prag?' 'A what?' 'A prag?' 'What on earth's that?' Somewhat aggrieved, the child explained:

'Well, when *I* upset something you tell me to go and fetch a damp rag, to mop it up.'

Ruth Williams, Devizes

320

Some years ago I was marking 11+ examination papers which included a vocabulary test. One question was: 'Write a word which describes a man who keeps on despite all difficulties.' An 11-year-old girl had given the answer:

'Passionate.'
Norman Wordsworth, Norwich

One of our nursery schools was performing its nativity play. The three wise men were offering their gifts to the baby in the manger when one of them forgot his lines. The teacher tried in vain to prompt him, but he was unreceptive. In desperation she told him: 'Just say anything then.' Whereupon the boy looked very closely at the baby and said:

'Isn't he like his Father!'
Millie Gresham, Limpsfield

In the middle of a service at a church I was worshipping in, a little boy – who turned out to be the vicar's son – shouted aloud to the elderly woman he was sitting next to:

'What colour are yours, Auntie?'
Revd Robert Ward, Moseley

'I've been given 70 years to live.'

A mother was trying to explain to her 4-year-old boy who Harold Pinter was: 'He's a very good writer.' The little boy looked up and said:

'Can he do a "W"?'

Small daughter Wendy:

'Oh, Auntie, I'm so glad you've arrived, 'cos Dad said that your turning up today was just what he needed!'

Tom Westman, Teangue

My inattentive 6-year-old daughter (many years ago) returned home from school after a scripture lesson, during the week before Easter:

'Mummy, people were very unkind to Jesus. They shouted, "Crucify him, crucify him!" Then they laid him on the grass to dry.'

Eleanor French, Falmouth

A goat we had – years ago – always accompanied us on our walks with the dogs. She loved eating blackberries. One day our 5-year-old daughter said pensively:

'Mummy, why does she *eat* black-berries and *do* blackcurrants?'

Margery and Maurice Humfrey,
Warminster

Keeping determinedly cheerful in the face of my 2-year-old being as cross and contrary as only a 2-year-old can be, I pointed out a thrush and said, 'Isn't that bird singing a beautiful song?' He looked at it sourly and said:

'It's not playing the piano.'

Mrs B. N. Jones, Hertford

Teacher: 'I wish you would pay more attention.'
Pupil: 'I'm paying as little as I can, sir!'

A 7-year-old daughter was watching her mother put on some face cream and asked, 'Mummy, is that the cream they show on the television that makes you beautiful?' When Mummy told her it was, she commented, after a thoughtful pause:

'It doesn't work very well, does it?'

On a bus from Bexhill three 10-year-old girls were talking about their schools and the topic as usual got round to school dinners. I overheard one of the girls ask what Grace the other two said before dinner. Without any hesitation they said:

'O, we say the same as the bride on her wedding day. "For what I am about to receive may the Lord make me truly thankful." '
Elizabeth Smith, Battle

Neighbour's daughter: 'We've an aunt coming to stay with us on my mother's side.'
Girl, aged 4: 'On your mother's side? Why? Doesn't she like your father?'

Two little girls were at the ballet. The smaller of the two turned to the other and asked, 'What are the big lumps for down the men's tights.' Replied the other:

'Don't be silly, they're for the ladies to stand on.'

My nephew, when a child, was introduced to the sea by his mother putting him in to paddle at the water's edge. Soon he came running back to her, saying:

'Mummy! It's too full.'
Elizabeth West, Brighton

A 6-year-old sustaining an argument with another who had declared that God did not exist:

'Of course there's a God. If there wasn't, they wouldn't put a van for him on all the trains.'
Mrs R. M. Farrer, Cheltenham

My husband gave our grandson Stephen – aged 4 – a bright new 10p piece. 'What do you say?' asked Grandad. Answered Stephen:

'One . . .'

Nora H. Bell, Harrow

WORD OF MOUTH

A friend ran a small boarding house and, on engaging a new housekeeper, warned her children to steer clear of the subject of husbands, as the lady had been married four times. At their first meal together, the 8-year-old son asked the housekeeper:

'What do you do with all your old wedding rings?'
Mrs P. E. Rautenbach, Warwick

My son when very small wheeled his toy donkey up to me. I saw that lined up on its back was a row of pennies. When I asked why, he replied:

'I'm putting money on a horse, like Daddy.'
Mrs H. Cook, Bristol

My daughter, aged 5, came home from school to say that one of boys had sworn at her. 'He called me a *boat*!' she said indignantly. 'But that's not swearing, dear,' I said gently. Came the reply:

'Oh no, not a *boat*. I remember now, he called me a *ship*!'
Mrs C. S. Barford, Bedford

326

A small boy was being bathed by his ample-bosomed granny. He peered down her cleavage as she knelt beside the bath. Said he:

'Granny, you've got your botty on backwards.'

After some misdemeanour, both my boys were blaming the other. I got very cross and sent them to their rooms until one of them owned up. Tea was ready and all was quiet, so I crept to the bottom of the stairs to find what progress was being made. I overheard the 5-year-old say to the 3-year-old:

'That's right, then? Heads you own up, tails I own up?'
Marie Brazier, Potters Bar

This is a saying from my husband's childhood which has become quite famous in our family. Question: 'Do you want this last piece of pie?' Answer:

'Not unless you want it.'
Jennifer Swinbank, Little Lever

My father is a clergyman and when my eldest brother was a small boy he apparently stood up in the middle of a sermon and declared:

'I think Daddy's said enough now!'
Roland Johnson, Westminster

Overheard outside the door of the room in which my 14-year-old son and his friends were having a candlelit seance:

'How long will I live? ... And will I have hairs on my chest?'
Jeanette Howarth, Swansea

Overheard by a village school teacher as two small boys from a nearby RAF station were talking. The first boy said, 'My Daddy can shoot ever so far, he could hit that tree.' The second boy claimed that *his* father could shoot higher. 'He shot right into the sky and up to Heaven.' First boy: 'Ooh – did it hit God?' Second boy, after a short pause:

'No, he wasn't at home.'
Mrs Betty Harrington, Aylesbury

Two small boys (about 8 years old) were hurrying by and one said:

**'Oh, his brother is very clever too ...
He can spell Czechoslovakia...'**
Marguerite Cluer, Truro

A mother was taking her son round an exhibition of abstract art and patiently trying to explain to him what it was all about. Said she pointing at one picture: 'And that's supposed to be a horse.' Said the boy:

'Well, why isn't it, then?'

Whilst teaching painting to a class of 7-year-olds I overheard a group of children discussing Adolf Hitler – what a nasty man he was and how he had personally shot six million people. I joined in the conversation, explaining that Hitler had in fact received some assistance with the killings. Then we were joined by another child who spoke these words:

'Hitler – isn't he the bloke with the wooden leg, the patch over one eye and a parrot on his shoulder?'

Long John Hitler!
David José, Muswell Hill

A child after church:

'Well, Auntie, I've been thinking over what you said about Lent, and I have decided to give up my cod-liver oil.'

Overheard by an elder sister – small person offering a bag of sweets to a friend:

'Take a lot. Take two.'

A small child hearing that God was everywhere inquired earnestly of his Mum, 'Is God in the loo?' 'Why, of course, dear,' was the reply, 'why do you ask that?' Said the boy:

'Because I heard Daddy say when he couldn't get in the loo, "My God, are you still in there?"'

My son, aged 8, was being shouted at one day through the bathroom door as others wanted to use the loo within the hour if possible. His immensely dignified reply, which has passed into family lore, was:

'I've started, so I'll finish.'
Mary Pascoe, London SW3

I overheard my 2-year-old daughter say to herself as she replaced the scissors:

'There, that didn't hurt the cat!'
Mrs K. M. Elcoate, Stafford

A child at prayer:

'Our Father, white shirts in heaven, Harold be thy name ...'

When I helped at a children's party, two little boys were talking about their baby sisters. Tommy said, 'My sister's got three teefs now.' The other little lad said:

'You don't say teefs – you say toofers.'
Mrs E. M. Hollingworth, Huddersfield

One day at lunch, our small son, Peter, still in his high chair, gave a loud belch. His father then a young assistant curate, put on a look of mock disapproval and demanded, '*What* do you say?' Peter, after a moment's thought, replied solemnly:

'Amen.'
Mrs P. M. Garman, Morpeth

'Mummy! Mummy! Daddy's

batteries have run out!'

WORD OF MOUTH

The 11-year-old daughter of a friend of mine was writing a comparison between the controversy over the 1980 Olympic Games in Moscow and the 1936 games in Berlin. She wrote that:

'Hitler expected his superior athletes to beat those from other races. But one marvellous black athlete disproved Hitler's theories by convincingly outstripping all his opponents. That black man's name was Jessie Matthews.'

Pamela Pamplin, Welling

When I was about 7 I came home from school one day and found that our daily woman was nowhere to be seen. My mother told me she had Housemaid's Knee. As I went to a convent and we were taught to pray, imagine my mother's hysterics when she heard me saying before I went to bed that night:

'Please, God, would you send me a Housemaid's Knee.'

Patricia Barrow, Bath

A married friend who lived alone with his daughter had a large collection of art books, ranging from the Italian primitives to the impressionists. Seeing all these on the shelves, a visitor asked the little girl, then about 4 years old, which of the artists she liked best. She replied:

'Oh, Jellybotty, he paints such lovely angels.'

Irene Oxley, Chiswick

In Manet's painting 'Le Déjeuner sur l'Herbe', only one of the picnickers – a lady – is entirely nude, for some inscrutable reason. A small American boy I met was shown the picture and after studying it remarked:

'You always forget something at a picnic.'

Miss M. H. Browne, London W14

The granddaughter of a friend interrupted her parents as they watched a nude scene on television. 'Mummy,' she said, 'That lady is very naughty.' The mother, apprehensively, asked why. The daughter:

'Well, she's going to bed without cleaning her teeth.'

D. Thom, Potters Bar

On her return from a party, a little girl was asked by mother whether she had remembered to say Thank You to the hostess. Rather alarmingly, the girl said she had not:

'The girl in front said Thank You and the lady said, "Don't mention it," so I didn't.'

Teacher: 'Victor's not feeling himself today.'
Pupil: 'Well, who is he then?'

As an ex-teacher, I recall a child of about 12 who was asked in an exam to give the story of Jesus and the Samaritan woman and said:

'Jesus met the Samaritan woman at a well. Jesus said unto the Samaritan woman, "How many husbands have you had?" and she, answering, said, "Lord, five." And Jesus said, "Give me a drink." '

Marion Chumbley, Twickenham

First little girl: 'My Mamma's hair is so long that she can sit upon it.'
Second little girl: 'But my Mamma can take hers off . . .'

336

My sons Mark and Dominic (7 and 5) proudly displayed their collection of model prehistoric monsters to a young visitor. 'That's a Stegasaurus, that's a Brontosaurus and that's a Tyrannosaurus Rex,' said the elder boy. Not to be outdone, the younger added:

'*And* we've got a *granny* upstairs.'
Victor Round, Stourbridge

My two daughters were watching the Queen during Trooping the Colour. Said one to the other:

'Oh, look – there's the lady that God saved.'
Wendy Evans, Dulwich

A little girl, aged about 5, was showing off her mother's dressing table things to another little girl of the same age. 'And this bottle is toilet water,' she explained. Said the other:

'In our house we would call it "lavatory" water.'
Cicely Denny, London SE7

One summer my 5-year-old son was getting excited about a cousin's wedding we were going to attend. We had already chatted about all the traditions of such an occasion. The night before the wedding, I was putting him to bed and as we talked, he said:

'And we're going to throw graffiti!'
Jennifer Eggleston, Long Ditton

During my 10-year-old son's music lesson, the teacher dictated to the class, 'His sighs grew with his ardour.' My son was extremely puzzled and asked:

'Is that spelt S-I-Z-E, sir?'
Mrs E. A. Cluley, Camberley

On being told that she now had a beautiful new baby brother, my 6-year-old daughter sighed and then remarked, quite politely:

'I would *rather* have had a bicycle.'
Mrs E. W. Malyon, Leigh-on-Sea

My 3-year-old son's comment on seeing his friend's new baby brother:

'We are going to have one of those – when Daddy can manage it.'
Jane Timms, Swindon

A little girl was found talking to nobody in the garden. 'What are you doing, darling?' her mother asked. Said the child:

'I'm talking to Aesop. I'm telling him a fable he doesn't know.'

I was at the house of a friend when a gentleman called to visit the father of the family who was out. The visitor was shown into the lounge to await his return. My friend's small sister followed him into the room and, after a few moments' scrutiny, demanded of him, 'Are you Dr Smith?' 'Yes, dear,' the visitor beamingly replied. After a perfectly timed pause the girl ventured to remark:

'My daddy says you cause nothing but trouble up at that golf club.'
Anne Marie Hawkins, East Molesey

An eavesdropping heard outside the junior section of the public library. Two little girls were talking and one remarked, 'Yes, we've moved into a house now, so me and my brother have got a bedroom each.' Then she added, thoughtfully:

'But Mummy and Daddy still have to share.'
Mrs E. Phillips, Barking

Opening the front door a few days before Christmas, I was asked by a boy of about 12 and his younger sister whether they could sing a carol. I explained that we had just had some carol singers a few moments before. 'Were they two girls, one wearing a blue anorak?' asked the girl. When I said they were, the boy exclaimed:

'That one was my cousin – I'll *kill* *her!*'

Mr W. V. Lush, Winchester

Sunday school teacher: 'What punishment did God inflict on Adam for eating the forbidden fruit?'
Little boy: 'He gave him a wife.'

My father was going to church one Sunday morning and decided to take my 5-year-old brother. It turned out to be a longer service than usual, the sermon having gone on for about forty minutes or more. My brother – to my father's everlasting embarrassment – suddenly piped up in a loud clear voice and asked:

'When is it half-time, Daddy?'
Miss F. M. Broughall, Preston

As a small boy, my brother was taken to Oxford Street, London, by our Austrian mother. A piper was marching up and down in the gutter as he played his instrument. My brother asked, 'Why does he walk up and down as he plays?' Mother said, 'I don't know, dear, I can't tell you.' After a pause for further thought, my little brother concluded:

'I expect he's trying to get away from the noise he's making.'
Claire J. Wrench, Ballaugh

My grandnieces are identical twins. On starting school their teacher was amazed at their similarity and asked, 'Doesn't your mother have trouble knowing which is which?' Said one of the twins:

'Oh no, we have different names.'
M. Smith, Edgbaston

A friend's daughter conversing with a little friend asked, 'Do you believe in the Devil?' Replied the other, somewhat scornfully:

'Of course not! It's like Santa Claus – it's Daddy.'
Mrs A. M. Rogerson, Sudbury

341

I have taught French for many years. I had occasion to discipline a boy for the second time in the same week. He had been told by his teacher to report to me, the headmaster, in my office. He was not very bright but he was keen on oral French. The interview ended with my saying to him, 'If you are reported to me again within the next fortnight, I shall cane you. Get out!' As he left my office, he said:

'Au revoir, monsieur.'
M. G. F. Le Blancq, Horndean

'We're playing mothers and fathers and he's got access to my doll at weekends.'

A mother asking her son after his first day at school if he liked it, received the reply:

'Yes. But I don't think I shall go very often.'

This is a conversation overheard by a friend of mine while sitting with her grandson aged $4\frac{1}{2}$ and his friend of the same age. The parents of this little boy were divorced and the father had access at weekends. The little friend asked the grandson:

'Whose is that photo?'
'It's my Grandad.'
'Where is he?'
'Up in heaven.'
'Where's that?'
'In the sky.'
'Garn!!!'
'Yes, he is. He was ill in hospital and they couldn't make him better, so God's taking care of him.'
'Does he come home at weekends?'
Mary F. Preece, Devizes

My daughter, Clare, when aged 4, asked her father:

'Daddy, if bees make honey, do wasps make marmalade?'
Betty McEntegart, Sheffield

WORD OF MOUTH

This was overheard on a bus. As two nuns descended from the upper deck, a small boy turned to his mother and cried:

'Mum, look, look – penguins!'

My 12-year-old grandson accompanied his mother to the Communion rail to receive a blessing but as the priest did not know if the boy had been confirmed, he bent down and whispered something in his ear. Then, to the mother's consternation, the priest administered the sacrament. When later on his mother asked the boy what had been said, he replied:

'He asked if I was Conservative and I said Yes.'
Kenneth Walker, Long Marston

I was frequently bossed about at school when younger. However, a friend and I once found *ourselves* ticking off a cheeky younger pupil who, as a parting shot, retorted, with great conviction:

'You *wait* till I'm older than you!'
R. M. F., Sheffield

Obviously very proud of his father, a small boy coming home from school on the bus, said, 'My dad hasn't half got a lot of hair on his chest.' To which his companion, not to be outdone, replied:

'So's my mum.'
J. Gunn, Chichester

Outside the Muswell Hill Odeon – a three-screen cinema – a minute but mutinous Thelwell-style girl, to her father:

'No, I want *The Stud* **or nothing.'**
Patrick Garry, Muswell Hill

Just after I had weaned my second baby, his 3-year-old brother burst into the room one day, stared at my top half and asked:

'Are you keeping those in case you have another baby?'
Mrs H. Brazier, Potters Bar

I was telling off my 3-year-old daughter and concluded by saying, 'When *are* you going to grow up?' The reply came:

'Next Saturday, I think.'
Mrs J. Wheatley, Clayton-le-Woods

WORD OF MOUTH

My daughter, aged 4, was patiently sitting in the back of the car while I drove and my husband map-read our way through a complicated German city. He did not appreciate it when I turned *left* when he had instructed me to turn *right*, but my daughter offered a practical solution:

'Daddy, why don't *you* drive and let Mummy shout at you.'
Vivien Womersley, Bath

I passed a bank cash point in time to see a man take delivery of some money. His young son was jumping up and down excitedly:

'Oh, Daddy, you were *very* lucky that time!'
Kathleen Kleboe, Othery

My daughter, Lois, during her formative years, was telling her slightly older brother to behave himself at the breakfast table. She said to him:

'Be quiet, Timothy, you know Daddy always listens to the apricot news.'
Stan Rodway, Kidlington

My wife Evelyn is very keen on country sayings and their meanings. A few years ago, we were driving along a country road near Loughborough when we passed a copse with a rookery in it. 'What does it mean when the rooks are resting high,' she asked our son Andrew, hoping for the reply, 'It means a good summer.' Said Andrew:

'It means they get a good view.'
Michael Treen, Gainsborough

When life with my two very young children reached a point of particular frustration one morning, I retired to the sitting room to calm down. I was soon conscious of being observed through a crack in the door. My 2-year-old son then returned to the kitchen and announced to his baby sister:

'Mummy's upset. I think she's teething.'
Patricia Wilkinson, Tonbridge

Heard outside my son's school: a mother asked her small son, 'Hullo, darling, had a good day?' Said the small son:

'Yes – but I haven't hit Richard yet.'
Mrs J. Williams, Teddington

347

I took my little girl to church for the first time and as we knelt in the tall-sided pew, she whispered:

'Who are we hiding from?'

My 4-year-old daughter, unable to remember the name of her favourite spread for breakfast toast, asked for:

'Bee jam, please.'
Alan Brooke, Bradford

When the subject of rows was brought up with my step-daughter, she said:

'Everybody has rows. If Pam's Mummy and Daddy didn't have rows, they would never talk to one another.'
Ian Middleton, Truro

A school howler that conjures up a bizarre image:

'Macbeth's courage failed him at the last minuet.'
Eileen Turner, Bridge of Allan

348

A small boy at prayer:

'And please send some clothes for those poor ladies in Daddy's magazines.'

Mother to 7-year-old son on seeing him suck his thumb: 'You promised to stop doing that on your seventh birthday.'
Son: 'Yes, I know, but it isn't easy giving up the habit of a lifetime.'

Lucille, aged 5, was sharing the bath with her younger sister Nicola. They were playing with a toy bat and Lucille started to explain that bats were blind. Nicola was most upset and wanted to know how they managed. Whereupon Lucille, anxious to console her sister, replied:

'Don't worry, Nicola, they manage very well as they have a fantastic sense of humour.'
Mrs A. Knighton Stephens, Winchcombe

Our 3-year-old daughter was spellbound during the christening ceremony of her baby brother. Her voice rang out loud and clear, reaching every member of the congregation:

'Why is the doctor putting David in that sink?'

Pamela Jackson, Gosport

My young grandson told me that I had left the door of the china cabinet with the key still in it. He added:

'But it's all right. I climbed up the bookshelves and put it on top, where I can't reach it.'

Stella Jowett, Middlesbrough

Christopher, now aged 2, was sitting on Grandma's knee, playing with the beads hanging around her ample bosom. 'Ooh,' he said. 'A big fat tummy.' A pause. Then:

'Ooh – *another* big fat tummy.'

Mrs Sheila Taylor, Sale

350

From a schoolboy's essay:

'An orchestra has a man – a Conductor – who stands out in front with a piece of paper which tells him what music the orchestra is playing.'

My nephew, then aged about 3, said, on discovering peaches for the first time:

'Ooh, look, Mummy – suede apples!'
Miss C. M. Moat, Cranbrook

When my daughter was 3 and my son 6, we were discussing the story of Noah and his ark. 'I know the animals went in two by two,' my son said. 'There was a female and her mate and the females had the babies.' I thought I knew what the next question would be but my daughter put in:

'The males were there to do the babysitting.'
Barbara Jukes, Loughborough

The vicar was at the church door as the congregation filed out after Morning Service. He saw a very small girl leave her mother's side and put two pence in the collecting box. Patting her head, the vicar said, 'That's a very nice and good thing to do, my dear.' She looked at him unsmiling and said:

'But nothing came out.'
Mrs F. S. Scott, Tisbury

A child at prayer:

'Shirley, good Mrs Murphy, shall follow me all the days of my life.'

My son, aged about $2\frac{1}{2}$, was watching me make a chocolate mousse for a dinner party and asked if he could have some. I replied No, it was for my friends in the evening. A little while later a hand crept round my leg and a voice said:

'Aren't I your friend?'
Prudence Meek, Ivybridge

Parent: 'Now, George, remember – the one who divides should always give the bigger half to the other.'
George: 'Bessy, you divide it.'

My sister when a toddler, *many* years ago, had just learned the Lord's Prayer at Sunday school. She was overheard at home repeating it delightedly to herself:

'Give us this day our daily bread and forgive us our Christmases.'
Jennie McKenna, Colchester

My wife once taught in a Roman Catholic primary school in Birmingham and overheard two small boys discussing what they'd just told the priest during their first confession. 'I couldn't think what to say,' said one. 'So I told him I'd stolen some money from my mom's purse, although I hadn't really.' 'But why didn't you tell him that you'd scratched "Aston Villa" on that desk?' suggested the other.

'You're joking! I'd get into trouble for that!'
Glenn O'Raw, Shirley

WORD OF MOUTH

'Why is it that you've never made one of those amusing remarks that other children make to keep their parents in stitches?'

A friend's little girl informed her mother that:

'The Equator is an imaginary lion which runs around the middle of the earth.'

Mrs L. J. Miller, Edinburgh

When I was in hospital having just given birth to a baby boy, my 6-year-old son, Andrew, was staying with friends. As he was going to bed in the evening having just seen his new baby brother, Andrew was heard to say to his friend Jonathan, 'Isn't God wonderful – God made everything.' After a long pause for thought, Jonathan replied:

'Yes, but Uncle Alan made the coffee table in the lounge.'
Ann Bagnall, Bletchley

I laughed haversacks when I heard this. A friend's kid said:

'Our new baby is a girl because her bottom goes all the way round.'
Evelyn Moon, St Osyth

My wife works in the local Zoological Museum and one day a family came in and were looking at the stuffed animals. The little girl asked, 'Do they bite?' to which her mother replied, 'Of course not, they're all dead.' Somewhat puzzled, the little girl asked:

'Have we come too late then?'
Martin A. Hendin, Tring

WORD OF MOUTH

I was teaching a third year class in religious studies. The lesson was about the Hindu caste system. I mentioned that in Hindu mythology the main castes are said to have been created from the body of Purusha, the first and eternal man. I explained that from Purusha's head came the intelligent, spiritual Brahmins; from his shoulders came the strong Kshatriyas, the warriors; from his thighs came the merchants and craftsmen, the Vaishyas; and from his feet the workers, the Sudras. All this time there was a boy in the front row whose eyes were getting wider and wider. Finally he could stand it no longer and exclaimed:

'Blimey, sir. What about the Untouchables?'

Eric Pain, Camberley

As the little boy was holding a packet of flower seeds in his hand, his mother decided that it was an opportune moment to tell him something of the Facts of Life. 'Darling,' she said, 'You grew from a tiny seed.' After a short pause for thought, the boy asked:

'Mummy, was there a picture of me on the packet?'

It so happened that a baby sister arrived for Jonathan on his birthday. But just prior to his next birthday, his mother told him: 'I'm sorry, dear, but you won't be getting a baby brother or sister this year. What would you like instead?' The boy replied:

'Well Mummy, if it wouldn't spoil your figure too much, I'd like a Shetland pony.'

Teacher: 'Where does cotton grow?'
Pupil: 'In Grandpa's ears.'

As we drove away from Hadrian's Wall, our youngest son, then aged 7, asked: 'Mummy, what's Barbara Ann?' I asked him what on earth he meant.

'Well, it says here in the leaflet that the Romans built Hadrian's Wall to keep out the Barbara Anns.'
Sue Massey, Crampmoor

An instance of my daughter Esther's logic! Out for a trip in a car, she was asked by way of observation and instruction, 'How many goats do you see in that field?' Esther answered:

'All of them!'
Mrs V. Eaves, Dawlish

357

'And what does *your* father do?'
'Oh my Daddy's a doctor.'
'So is mine. Where does your Daddy practise?'
'Oh, my Daddy doesn't practise, he's a *proper* doctor.'

At the bus-stop, a lady was telling another one about a forthcoming happy event in the family and said that her son had suggested the name Thomas if it was a boy and his wife had said she would like to call it Ruth if it was a girl. To which the woman's granddaughter had added:

'And if it's a dog can we call it Casey?'
Lee Bramzell, Billericay

Our 3-year-old daughter was very disappointed when we told her that her favourite TV programme was not on. A few minutes later, however, the News began and a dramatic picture of Michael Foot appeared on the screen. She cried:

'Oh, look, it *is* The Muppets!'
Jenny and Colin Baines, Kings Heath

During 1942, I took my eldest daughter, then aged 4, into the old village church at Woolston, Gloucestershire. Drawing her attention to the stained glass window behind the altar which showed a figure of Jesus with a saint standing on either side of him, I said: 'That is gentle Jesus.' Looking at the two saints, my daughter asked:

'Who are those two – Meek and Mild?'
T. Eastwood, Odemira, Portugal

Some years ago we took my daughter (a country child) to market with her cousin (a town child), both about 7 years old. Our niece asked: 'What's the difference between a cow and a bull?' Our daughter answered:

'A cow gives you milk and bull gives you Bovril.'

Very recently my 3-year-old granddaughter came up to me and gave me a great big hug and said:

'I do love you, Grandma. Will you be my sister?'
Kathleen J. Brewin, Shaftesbury

My husband was watching our 6-year-old daughter doing a colouring competition when she turned to him and said, 'I shan't win this competition.' My husband replied: 'Come on, Philippa, don't be negative about it, try and be positive.' To which she said:

'I'm *positive* **I shan't win the competition.'**

Susan Smith, Lichfield

My wife Jill is a teacher. She overheard two girls in the dinner queue discussing a member of staff who was about to have a baby. One was in the process of telling the other in a very knowledgeable way:

'If Mrs Jones doesn't have her baby soon, I expect she'll have to be seduced.'

Roger Walkinton, Lewes

Definitely a sign of our times: I asked my 10-year-old son if he had had any lessons yet about growing up. He thought a moment and then said:

'Do you mean like learning to sign on?'

Diana Skelt, Gainsborough

'Now, this is what I want
next Christmas.'

WORD OF MOUTH

Two small daughters in the bath. One inquired: 'Mummy, what does striptease mean?' I explained as succinctly as I felt befitted their years, but the debate must have continued while I went out of the bathroom to fetch something, since on my return I heard the younger one gasp:

'You mean they take their *vests* off!'
Janet Salway, Bristol

My friend and I took her young son round our local church and he became very noisy. 'Hush,' my friend said, 'You are in God's house. You mustn't shout.' Said her indignant son:

'Why not? If God came to my house, I'd let *him* shout.'
Joanna Taylor, Nottingham

My 2-year-old son was most interested in his baby brother and delighted in watching me bath the baby. As I started to breast-feed, he wanted to know what I was doing. 'Giving the baby his breakfast,' I said. Pause for thought. Then:

'Does he have cereal from one side and toast from the other?'
Beryl St John, Bridport

362

When I was at school, the teacher quoted 'Vanity of vanities' from the Bible and asked someone to complete the quotation. Immediately, one small crawler shot up his hand and uttered this memorable completion:

'Vanity of vanities, all is vanity – except the teacher.'
Nellie K. Poole, Plumstead

Having just learned to read, my 5-year-old daughter was busily reading all the shop signs in town. Passing a gentlemen's out-fitters, she excitedly announced:

'That's right, isn't it, mummy – *men swear* **– they do swear, don't they?'**
Mrs P. Holt, Kendal

A small boy in the greengrocer's was standing behind me in the queue. As I was collecting my purchases, the boy was heard to ask for:

'Five elubs of potatoes, please.'

So much for decimalisation. I suppose he meant 'lbs'.
Margaret Needham, Kilmarnock

WORD OF MOUTH

During a conversation round the dinner table, the subject of singers and pop groups came up. I remarked that some had no talent and were only in it for the money – with which my daughter Imogen, aged 6, agreed, and added:

'Look at carol singers, for instance.'
Elizabeth Luddy, Nottingham

Teacher: 'Stop acting the fool, Gray.'
Gray: 'I'm not acting, sir!'

My daughters Jill, aged 6, and Sally, 4, had spent the day with their grandmother. They came home excitedly chattering about how they had spent the afternoon dressing up from a sack of old clothes. Sally's favourite had been a bra which she described to us as having frilly straps over the shoulders, a hook at the back to fasten it:

'... and little flowers on the points where the nibbles go.'
N. J. Nichols, Llandyssul

A class of girls at a convent school was asked to write an essay on 'The Joys of Youth'. One little girl having given a list of the joys of youth ended with the line:

'These are just some of the Joys of Youth, but, oh, for the Joys of Adultery!'